RELUCTANT MESSENGER

· RETURNS ·

AN UNEXPECTED ADVENTURE INTO THE ANGELIC REALM

Candice M. Sanderson

CLARK
PRESS

An Imprint of Crystalline Wisdom Path, LLC
Naples, Florida

Parties interested in quantity sales or autographed copies may contact Clark Press through the author's webpage at www.CandiceSanderson.com.

CLARK
PRESS

Published by Clark Press, Naples, Florida
Clark Press is an imprint of Crystalline Wisdom Path, LLC

Cover design by MaryDes Designs
Interior design and formatting by MaryDes Designs
Editorial assistance by Eleanore Zurbruegg
Author photo by Dr. Neil Cohen

The Reluctant Messenger Returns:
An Unexpected Adventure into the Angelic Realm
by Candice M. Sanderson
First Edition
10 9 8 7 6 5 4 3
Library of Congress Control Number: 2020908298

ISBN 978-0-9996427-3-3 (pbk)
ISBN 978-0-9996427-4-0 (ebook)
ISBN 978-0-9996427-5-7 (hdbk)

To Lorelai Lee and Shalane Grace

May you always believe in magic!

TABLE OF CONTENTS

the
RELUCTANT MESSENGER
· RETURNS ·

AN UNEXPECTED ADVENTURE INTO THE ANGELIC REALM

CHAPTER 1
HINDSIGHT - A NEW BEGINNING
May 2020

O ver the course of a few short weeks in early 2020, life as we had known it disappeared. The novel coronavirus swept our planet, wreaking havoc in its wake. As the disease became a pandemic, fear spread across the Earth as countries issued lockdown orders. Unless deemed an essential worker, law mandated us to go inside.

Going inside is what would save us. I'm not referring to the wisdom and data from the scientists and medical communities. Certainly, sheltering in place reduces the spread of COVID-19, but this is the same advice from our angels and guides.

Seven years had passed since my spontaneous opening to the unseen world of the nonphysical, and I had become accustomed to conversing with angels, guides, and many others who inhabit their realms. Now it's easy to make those statements; after all, I had compiled reams of countless messages I'd verified through after-the-fact research. At the time, however, it wasn't easy; it challenged me. Although my training as a psychologist had taught me to trust only what I could measure with my physical senses, the data I collected transformed me from skeptic to believer. More than that, I've learned to follow the advice from my nonphysical friends.

As I look at our world in May 2020, the messengers I've trusted have told me to go within; that is where we will find answers. The angels said the pandemic represents a reset for Gaia, the spirit of Mother Earth. Now is a time to embrace unity.

As we sink into the silence of our hearts, we realize we stand on the precipice of this new post-pandemic landscape. We are like butterflies, preparing to emerge from our chrysalises into a new horizon. A year ago, the angels said humanity was at a tipping point as our planet prepared to enter a cycle that would raise her vibrations into higher dimensional realms.

There's no handbook to navigate these unprecedented times. But as we teeter on the brink of this new world, we're not left to our own devices. The angels are here to assist.

It won't happen immediately; it will happen in stages. As we cross the post-pandemic threshold, some will move into the new frequencies faster than others, becoming the trailblazers for us to follow.

These higher vibrations will thin the veils between the physical and nonphysical worlds, and many will begin to connect to the realms of angels and guides. We'll understand our relationships to all living things as we seek the cosmic memories that had united us since before time existed. We will embrace humanity as one; we are family, linked as brothers and sisters across the globe.

Throughout the past seven years, I've seen a pattern unfold from the messages. Overarching themes of unity, transformation, and hope emerge, but more recently, there have been indications of a change coming to our Earth. I've heard a clarion call for action as our planet enters an evolutionary phase of transformation.

Many messages from both this and my first book, *The Reluctant Messenger~Tales from Beyond Belief*, become more relevant and significant when viewed through the lens of the COVID-19 pandemic. These are no longer simply philosophical messages wrapped in poetic language, hinting of evolutionary changes. The events they foretold are happening now, in real time.

Yet we are not alone. The messengers advise us, showing us roadmaps to navigate during these unprecedented times. They speak of their continual guidance, preparing us to cross the threshold into the future.

I offer an example: In mid-August 2019, a storm had whipped through the area during the wee hours of the morning, but by seven, crisp blue skies had replaced the dark clouds and wind. The weather was ideal for a beach walk. As I stepped on the rain-soaked sand, my eye caught a beautiful rainbow arcing across the quiet waters of the Gulf of Mexico.

I felt the gentle nudge from the nonphysical realm, so I opened my phone to record the message. There was wisdom in the words they shared, but a more significant meaning emerged in May 2020, as I was preparing this manuscript for publishing.

The August 2019 message indicated our world would undergo a significant change. Little did we know a few months later, an insidious respiratory disease from across the planet was about to change our lives. Amid global lockdowns, fear is rampant, and anxieties skyrocket as the death toll rises. As unemployment surges, panic fills the hearts of many. The messengers had been right; these events changed the world as we knew it.

But there is hope. We are not alone; the angels are here to guide us. Life is a web of events, woven across the fabric of time with actions overlaid by circumstances. Does our past determine our future? The angels urge us to look at life through a changed perspective, one where humanity can travel together for the common good.

Let's not let the narrow thinking of others chart our path. Let us work together to weave hope and truth into the tapestry of our lives as we prepare to enter these unknown territories of a post-pandemic world.

I invite you to hear the words of the angels as they spoke of these things, months before our world changed:

August 14, 2019

Do you not see the wisdom of the rainbow? Do you not see the promise that has been given since Biblical times? It is the promise of unity, the promise of oneness.

The rainbow brings a different perspective to light. It calls forth the invisible to the visible realm, producing the sacred arc of the rainbow. The colors within it are defined, yet they are still only one. They operate in unison, not as separate energies that veer in different directions, but as one, as the integration of all there is.

A new light is coming upon the Earth plane, and it is changing the world as you know it. But like the prism that brings the rainbow into view, you also need a new perspective. Think not of the discord and disharmony in the world that surrounds you but learn to view life with a different lens.

The truth lies in your path. Breathe deeply, Dear Ones, and bring hope and light back into your existence. Know that true magic lies at the end of the rainbow where the past melds with the future, and duality no longer exists. This is where humanity travels together for the common good, a common goal.

Lift up thine eyes and see the beauty that surrounds you. Embrace this truth.

As Mother Earth transitions, she brings us new light. We can huddle in the darkness of fear or choose the light of introspection. Will we lift our eyes and see the promise of a new world, a better world? Will we come into alignment and travel as one into this new horizon? I certainly hope so.

C. S. Lewis said, "You can't go back and change the beginning, but you can start where you are and change the ending." Will we do that now? Will the foresight of the angels offer us the 2020 vision of hindsight? Years from now, I hope we'll look at life on our marvelous blue-green planet and know we made the right choices, and that 2020 was, indeed, the year of perfect vision.

CHAPTER 2: MIRACLES HAPPEN

My life transformed one morning in late summer 2013, and the world as I had known it dissolved in front of my eyes. As a psychologist, my senses grounded me in the physical; if I could not measure something, it didn't exist. Everything changed on August 28, 2013, when I began receiving messages from other-worldly sources.

Visions often accompanied these specific and detailed communications from spirit. Sometimes the information arrived instantly, fully downloading into my awareness within seconds. Other times, the knowledge came like dictation. I not only knew what words to use, but where to place quotation marks, start a new paragraph, capitalize letters, insert parentheses, and what punctuation to use.

The onslaught of these communications surprised me. I didn't understand how or why these messages arrived, so I relied on my training as a psychologist and began to document the information. My initial skepticism faded with each search-engine hit, verifying evidence I had collected. Day after day and message by message, I learned to trust what I had received.

For most of my life, I had been a psychologist. It's where my confidence came from; it's how I defined myself. Initially, it was hard to let those pieces of me go, but then I realized none of what defined me before defines me now. I smiled as I recognized I had exchanged that predictable and secure existence for a life filled with wonder, awe, and perhaps a little magic.

I retired in June 2018, replacing my psychologist's shingle with an author's pen. By the end of the month, I had published *The Reluctant Messenger~Tales from Beyond Belief*, a book chronicling my spontaneous spiritual awakening. It had taken courage to share personal experiences in such a public forum, but it outweighed the risks, so I accepted another challenge; I would write a children's spiritual manual. This second book was well underway, but that was about to change.

The Reluctant Messenger had gained attention from the spiritual and metaphysical communities, and I'd received invitations to participate in several interviews. On October 24, 2018, I was a visitor on Joe Rupe's program, *Lighting the Void* on The Fringe FM, an Internet radio station. Joe's guests come from all walks of life with interests ranging from the esoteric and paranormal to science and pop culture.

I didn't know at the time, but during a break in the interview, my children's book became sidetracked when Joe shared a fascinating story. He described an encounter during his early teens with what he thought might have been an angel. As he detailed the event, cold chills racked my body. Chills have always been my sign that something important is happening, and I should pay attention.

I had questions. It wasn't about whether the man who had come to Joe's miraculous rescue was an angel. I knew he was. In the back of my mind, I wondered why Joe had shared this personal story. Was this a message for me? What was the deeper meaning behind this break-time conversation? Had this been orchestrated by the messengers?

Shortly after the interview, I felt a nudge to put the children's book aside; the following day, the push became stronger. On the third day, I was ready to listen. For reasons I wouldn't discover until later, I knew I needed to write about angels, these divine beings who protect us and, like Joe's encounter, bring miracles into our lives.

Later that week, I sat at my computer and began to organize material for this new adventure. *The Reluctant Messenger* had a chapter on angels called *Heavenly Help*, but I needed fresh content. (For interested readers, I've included *Heavenly Help* in the Bonus section at the back of the book.)

New material arrived the next day. While on an early morning nature walk, a door to the angel realm opened, bringing more messages. I turned off my phone's music app and, using the built-in microphone on my earbuds, began recording.

Later that night, I sat at my computer, preparing to transcribe the previous week's messages from my phone and my notebook. I was surprised when I opened the journal. At the top of the page was an invocation, inviting angels to "bring forth their loving energy so others may have a taste of the divine that I feel when they surround me."

I glanced at the date above this handwritten memo. It was several days before my conversation with Joe on Lighting the Void. A wave of cold chills engulfed me as I realized why I had no memory of writing these words. This message was not from our three-dimensional world. No, its genesis was from a much grander source—angels.

My eyes crinkled into a smile, and I sighed with relief. Just like Joe's story, the angels were here to rescue me, too. They would assist on this journey as I penned my encounters with them. Once I began this new endeavor, information flowed into my awareness like water bursting from a dam. The angels revealed ancient secrets, resulting in new insights for me. Hope and promise for a brighter future surfaced, and it had begun with Joe's story during a break in the podcast.

I learned angels had accompanied me at birth, and I savored their promise to escort me when it's my time to leave. I began to recognize the various ways they had influenced me, sometimes subtly, sometimes not. Their reappearance in my life was too intense to ignore. The angels had reawakened my passion for life, for hope, for miracles.

Pushing aside the manuscript I had intended to write, I began this book instead. I hope my encounters with these angelic beings might provide some insight or comfort for others. My contact with them has reassured me that they protect us. It was now my time to acknowledge the importance they held for me.

The true reason for writing this book didn't wink into view until a few weeks before this memoir's scheduled publication date in spring of 2020. The world scrambled for answers. More than ever before, we needed reassurance that angels are with us as we navigated the unchartered territories of a global pandemic.

As COVID-19's mortality rate increased astronomically across the globe, we pleaded for a miracle. Would that provide the answers we sought? I smiled and nodded as I realized how my connection to the world of the nonphysical had begun. Only recently had I realized a miracle had been the doorway to my unexpected adventure into the angelic realm.

It was February 2013. I rushed from the doctor's office before anyone could see the tears welling in my eyes. More surgery? The last operation had created this problem, but I had to do something. I had lived for three months with a paralyzed vocal cord, and it wasn't getting better. I couldn't speak louder than a whisper, and I couldn't drink liquids without choking. My life was miserable.

I needn't have worried. A miracle occurred a few days later, and I was healed.

For as long as I can remember, I've carried a notebook to jot down important dates, make to-do lists, or document items I didn't want to forget. As passages from the messengers became longer and more frequent, I began to use my phone to record these words of wisdom. My notepad was always there as a backup when this was not possible.

As words of inspiration flowed into my awareness, I recorded them with ease. Most times, I would transcribe these communications the night I received them, but every once in a while, one would go unnoticed.

When I least expected but often needed them, these unanticipated words would find their way into my awareness. This was never truer than a message I had recorded on Valentine's Day 2013 but not discovered until five-and-one-half years later.

This message became a pivotal point in my life. Although I was initially surprised at the delay in discovering the recording, I later understood why it had taken so long to reach me. I had to meet specific criteria before I could comprehend its meaning.

I may have forgotten about the voice memo, yet, I could never forget the surrounding circumstances. It was an uncomplicated surgery, but the quick in and out to remove the diseased thyroid turned out to be not-so-typical. Surgical complications from the November 2012 bilateral thyroidectomy resulted in paralysis of my right vocal cord, and my once-loud voice became a whisper. As a psychologist whose career involved speaking, this created quite the dilemma. I found a quick and efficient resolution through a voice amplification system.

I used a microphoned headset that projected my voice through an external speaker that hung on my belt or a lanyard around my neck. The contraption was cumbersome, but it worked. I embraced the technology through curtains of humiliation and embarrassment. I had no choice. Without my voice, I could not perform my duties as a psychologist.

At the time, I was working with elementary-aged students, and I wondered whether my new look might frighten them. So, with a sense of excitement to capture their attention, I introduced my new voice system.

Students love electronic devices, and they were fascinated to hear my microphoned whispers echo across the office. It was a success, and many pleaded to use it. Before long, the novelty wore off, and I was able to assume my duties as usual.

Fast-forward to February 2013. It was three months post-surgery and obvious my voice would not return without help from a specialist. My surgeon referred me to an otolaryngologist, a physician who specializes in the ear, nose, and throat.

The doctor inserted a flexible camera-tipped scope through my numbed nose and down my throat to view my vocal cords. With eyes on the video's monitor, he maneuvered the tube deep into each fold of both vocal cords while I repeated sound patterns.

As he inched the scope along the interior of my throat, the camera felt like it was expanding, and I had increased difficulty breathing. Although numbing my nasal cavity and throat helped, the process was increasingly uncomfortable; minutes felt like hours. Just when I felt a panic attack was imminent, the procedure ended, and the doctor retracted the tube. Its removal was as painful as its insertion.

The doctor confirmed what my surgeon and I already knew: I had a paralyzed vocal cord. In the remaining minutes, he recommended a surgical implant in the larynx to help reposition the damaged area. The proposed treatment weighed heavily on my mind, but I knew I could no longer go through my life attached to a microphone and speaker.

Handing me my file for checkout, the physician instructed me to return the following week to begin the pre-surgical process. I gave the receptionist my chart, and she collected my insurance co-pay. She squinted to decipher the doctor's handwritten notes, then looked at me over the rims of her reading glasses and asked whether I preferred a morning or afternoon appointment for the following Wednesday.

The prospects of another surgery terrified me, and I couldn't regain my composure enough to book the appointment. I whispered I was going out of town for the weekend, and I'd schedule when I returned. I never made that call.

On Friday, February 15, 2013, I hopped on a plane to Charlottesville, Virginia, not knowing what would happen that weekend, not knowing how my life would forever be changed. I was oblivious that I had taken my first step toward a miracle. I disembarked and headed to the airport's lobby to find a familiar face. We'd take the forty-minute trip by van to Monroe Institute, where I would co-host a working retreat.

The institute is world-renowned for its studies in consciousness exploration through sound-based technologies, and I was a founding member of their volunteer wing, the Local Chapter Network. My hands were full as we hosted approximately fifty in-house guests, plus those who attended through our live-streaming platform. Having spent hundreds of hours planning this event, we were excited and ready to begin. We would be announcing our grass-roots initiative to share Monroe Institute's technology across the globe.

Fitting me with microphones was challenging. My pre-surgical voice would have been more than sufficient to handle a room of fifty people, but now I needed amplification. The familiar screech of audio feedback let me know when my voice speaker was too close to the in-house mic. After several minutes of trial and error, we decided on two microphones: I'd use the personal amplification system for inhouse and a separate mic for online streaming. We were ready for the final soundcheck.

I looked over the crowd while the staff arranged the cameras and made other preparations for broadcasting. Monroe Institute has always drawn an exciting mix of participants, including spiritually minded psychologists, medical doctors, physicists, and scientists from different fields. I knew there were several natural healers in both the online and on-campus audiences.

Shortly after introducing myself and welcoming everyone to the event, I briefly explained the cause of my distorted voice, and I issued an invitation for healing energies. I tried to ignore the upcoming surgery, but it loomed in the back of my mind like a wild animal, and I was its prey. My heart raced every time I thought of another operation.

My request, in retrospect, had carried me closer to healing. Intentions are powerful, and my desire to be whole started a chain of events that would unfold over the next few days. Unaware, I had just edged closer to a miracle.

During a break, a couple of members from the audience approached me to offer a healing session. I sighed deeply, and with tears springing to my eyes, I humbly accepted.

I went to the lower level of the institute's Nancy Penn Center at the arranged time and headed toward a massage table in the center of the room. I smiled when I saw the majority of the workshop attendees present. They formed a circle near the perimeter of the room, holding sacred space for me while the two primary healers, Fred and Carol, administered the energies.

When the session ended, I brought my hands to my chest in a prayer position and bowed to the group, giving my heartfelt thanks. I went straight to bed. It was early, but I was tired and sleepier than usual. Had the healing exhausted me, or was I fatigued from helping to facilitate the retreat? Perhaps it was both.

Daylight slipped through the gaps between the darkened bed curtains, landing squarely on my face and waking me from my peaceful slumber. I stood to greet the sun. Patches of mist quilted the sides of the Blue Ridge Mountains. I opened the frosted windowpane, and the brisk morning nipped at my face. This was a different world from my subtropical home in Naples, Florida.

I took a deep breath, smiling as I realized I was at one of my favorite places in the world, stitched securely inside this mountain retreat. I slipped on my robe and headed down the stairs toward the smell of coffee.

Within minutes, people drifted toward the sounds in the kitchen, telling us breakfast was near. I was ready for Saturday's action-packed schedule. The last full day of the retreat was the following day, and we had a special event planned. We would be beta testing a newer version of one of the institute's sound-based technologies, Spatial Angle Modulation™, also known as SAM.

At lunch on Sunday, we announced the SAM product testing would take place after the day's final event. We were fans of Monroe Institute and eager to experience these newer SAM frequencies, plus we knew our feedback would help their research.

We explained the process. The participants would return to their assigned rooms where they would listen to three short audio samples through headsets. We scheduled sufficient time between each selection for everyone to document anecdotal findings and complete a brief survey. When the exercises ended, we would reconvene in David Francis Hall to return the paperwork and debrief.

A ten-minute break for staff to load the selections into the system gave everyone sufficient time to return to their rooms and prepare. I was eager to participate, but little did I know the impact this event would have on me.

As I listened to the second selection, colorful hypnagogic images of swirling colors rising like early-morning mist played before my closed eyes, giving everything a dreamlike quality. I felt as though I was falling in slow motion. I drifted on clouds of peaceful surrender.

The silhouette of a man approached me. As he drew closer,

I realized I was face-to-face with the great spiritual teacher and religious leader, Buddha. Looking directly in my eyes, he made one statement, "Be silent for twenty-four hours, and you will be healed."

Was this real? Had Friday night's healing circle created this? I did not know, nor did I care. I was going to honor the request; I vowed not to speak for twenty-four hours.

While the participants returned to David Francis Hall to discuss our findings, I scribbled my experience in my journal. I yearned to share my thoughts, but I would not break my vow of silence. I handed my scrawled notes to the person next to me, requesting she share it with the group.

As she read my findings, I relived the event in my mind. Oh, how I wanted to explain my surprise when I saw and heard Buddha speak. I desperately wanted to tell everyone that I had no affinity to him or Buddhism.

I wished I could shout that this was not a figment of my imagination, for if it had been, I would have chosen a messenger common to my Christian heritage. Buddha? He wasn't even in my orbit, so I knew the communication had not come from me. There was so much I wanted to say, but I would not break my silence.

Most of the participants gathered in the Fox Den for an evening snack. We munched on popcorn and chips, discussing our plans to build local chapters in our respective homes. Voices stopped mid-sentence as familiar chimes of incoming text messages pinged throughout the room, sending some scrambling to find their phones. As I read my text, I sighed. A snowstorm caused the cancellation of all early-morning outgoing flights. In the back of my mind, I wondered whether this was a test for me.

Everyone at the retreat knew of my vow of silence. When I showed my text to a friend along with a jotted plea for assistance, he graciously agreed to help. As he spoke with airline personnel, I stood close by and scribbled any information needed for the flight change. This coordinated effort paid off. Although delayed by twelve hours, I finally had a ticket home.

This silence-for-twenty-four-hours pact was challenging, and I couldn't help but wonder whether it was part of the bigger picture. Was this a measure of my endurance, my commitment? Whether it was or it wasn't, I was eager to test my voice.

I flew home, all the while keeping an eye on the clock as the minutes crept by. Twenty-four hours passed and my heart pounded as I reached the moment of truth. I started with just a sound, not even a word. I could not believe my ears. Not only could I speak, I had full volume. I felt elated as I shouted for joy at the miracle that had occurred.

This mysterious event defied logical explanation. Yes, it was a miracle, but that begged the questions of why and how. How was I healed? Which phenomenon had healed me? Was it the intention behind my request for help that kick-started the process? Had it been the healing circle, Buddha, or the SAM technology? Was it a combination of all of these?

I did not know how the healing had occurred, only that it had, and I realized the power of these phenomena could change people's lives. Who are we to judge the validity of something so transformative, just because we cannot explain it?

Without realizing it, I held the answers. Like a secret neatly tucked away, years passed before I discovered the truth. A sudden understanding more significant than words came forth, and I realized spirit had silently orchestrated these events, and its purpose was about to be revealed.

It was August 2018 and past time to upgrade my cell phone. As I backed up old data in preparation for the new purchase, I found an untitled voice memo with a timestamp of February 14, 2013. I tapped the play button and listened to my artificially amplified voice: "It is Valentine's Day, and I am driving to work. I am being told that the reason behind my challenges with my voice is that I need to become the voice of a channel. I am surrounded by love; I am surrounded by angels. Only by silencing my voice am I able to tap into those energies that have been approaching me for some time. By silencing my voice, I can become the voice of those who need to be heard. These are the voices of healing, the voices of love that need to be shared with all. From this point on, I shall remember this and speak from heart-based love."

I chuckled as I listened to my whispered voice, stating I would remember the message. Wrong. I had no memory of the recording, even though my miraculous healing occurred only three days later. For reasons I would soon learn, it was to remain hidden in the recesses of my memory.

The reason for the lag between the 2013 Valentine's Day recording and its discovery in August 2018, eventually became apparent, and it offered a sense of clarity. With the unearthing of this monumental voice memo came the realization I had held the answers all along. Yet, before I could understand the message, several prerequisites were required, and those conditions had taken five and one-half years to transpire.

The first requirement was my three-month-long nightmare with no voice. It wasn't just the vocal cord paralysis; my life changed. I quickly learned vocal cords did more than produce sound. They prevent food and drink from entering the trachea and causing coughing spasms or choking.

I avoided thin liquids, but I needed to stay hydrated in the South Florida heat. I realized if I allowed only a few drops of water to trickle down my throat, I could prevent aspiration—most of the time. Even the simple act of swallowing little amounts of saliva could be dangerous, so I tried to make all drinking or eating a concerted, practiced effort.

When I would choke, my face turned crimson as I struggled to breathe. My forced attempts to gasp for air quickly silenced any room. Whether at a restaurant or in a class of students, all eyes turned to me, and the looks on their faces revealed I wasn't the only one frightened.

These episodes paled in comparison to my nights when I had no conscious control over swallowing. A swift round of asphyxiation would catapult me from my peaceful sleep. This cycle of swallowing-choking-panic resulted in many sleepless nights.

I knew how strange I looked and sounded using a mechanical voice apparatus. I felt humiliated, but how else could I perform my job? My voice was my lifeline; I needed it to survive.

The voice enhancement system enabled me to continue working as a psychologist. The device amplified my whispers, but I would become breathless if I spoke too much. I tried not to let my friends, family, and coworkers know how much this affected me, but I cried myself to sleep most nights. I felt drained, and the situation was taking its toll on me. After three months, reality set in, and I knew this was not going away. I scheduled an appointment for medical intervention.

Struggling with the three-month-long vocal cord nightmare had been the first prerequisite for comprehending the Valentine's Day message. The second prerequisite was the miraculous healing at Monroe Institute.

I had taken my voice for granted. I had used it every day from the moment I was born until November 2012. I never expected to lose it. I discovered the truth behind the phrase about not knowing what you've got until it's gone.

After honoring Buddha's request at Monroe to remain silent for twenty-four hours, my first vocalizations were music to my ears. I felt so much gratitude for this inexplicable healing that I dropped to my knees. I cried when I realized I had experienced a miracle.

I had crossed the first two hurdles: three months without my normal voice, followed by healing. Yet another obstacle blocked my path to discovering and understanding the Valentine's Day message. This final puzzle piece was significant because it foretold the reason for my vocal cord nightmare—I was to become a voice for those without one. That was unfathomable to me in 2013. Yet, as I listened to the Valentine's Day recording, I realized my post-surgical challenges had granted me access to energies that would transform me into a messenger. I would become a voice for the angels. Two months before discovering this hidden recording, I had done precisely that. I had shared their words of wisdom by publishing *The Reluctant Messenger~Tales from Beyond Belief.* I had unwittingly fulfilled the angel's request to become the channel they had predicted so many years before.

I sat at my computer to transcribe this long-forgotten recording into my online journal, and as this last puzzle piece fell into place, I smiled so broadly my cheeks hurt. I finally understood the reason for the delay in discovering this prophetic voice memo. Everything the angels had said in the Valentine's Day message had come to fruition: my vocal-cord paralysis, the miraculous healing, and me becoming a voice.

Discovering the recording was a game-changer for me, and the impeccable timing of the message had me shaking my head in disbelief. The key to understanding my miraculous healing had surfaced in this neatly tucked-away recording that arrived on the universal day of love, Valentine's Day.

As I look back at the 2013 miracle, I feel overcome with feelings of love and gratitude. I know angels surround us, and I'm confident they work their magic in ways we cannot begin to comprehend. Angelic forces worked behind the scenes at Monroe Institute for me to reclaim my voice.

Unbeknownst to me, the angels had orchestrated the events to manifest my miracle, and I had unwittingly become an integral part of this process that changed my life. Could I uphold my end of the bargain? Would I be able to share the voices of healing and love from the angels? I pondered these rhetorical questions, and although I did not know the answers, I took a deep breath and smiled. Their miraculous healing had changed me, and I knew, without a doubt, I was I willing to try.

CHAPTER 3: THERE AND BACK AGAIN

Nowhere to hide. How do I escape? I tried to yell, but there was nothing but painful silence.

This recurring theme invaded my dreams from November 2012 until my miracle in mid-February 2013. It mimicked the real-life panic I felt during those three months with a paralyzed vocal cord.

I thought about my healing and sighed deeply as I realized those nightmares were over. I had avoided a painful and costly surgery, and I experienced something that no one I knew had encountered—a bona fide medical miracle. Without a doubt, the spontaneous recovery of my paralyzed vocal cord had altered my life. Yet, more than five years later, discovering the preordained nature behind these life-transforming events was equally astonishing.

The Valentine's Day message not only explained the reasons behind my post-surgical condition but also foretold future events. When I recorded these prophetic words, little did I know the return of my voice was to serve another purpose. I was to become a spokesperson for other-dimensional beings. I slipped into the prelude to my speaker's role six months later as I drove to work in August 2013.

With the prophesized message predicting these events wiped

from my memory, other-worldly communications flooded into my awareness during an early morning commute. I was too shocked and astounded to judge what was occurring, so I reverted to my clinical training as a psychologist and documented my findings. Over time, I grew accustomed to these paranormal conversations. As I look back at my initial fears, I realize there was nothing scary about this at all; it was magnificent.

When the spiritual floodgates opened, souls who had crossed that great divide we call death contacted me. I received messages from star systems, guides, ascended masters, and angels. I learned valuable lessons, such as how to use worry and anxiety as opportunities for spiritual growth. The messengers taught me about time and how it worked. They showed me how energy connects everything and how you could manipulate it to heal others.

Eventually, these messages assimilated into my every-day life. Although I continued to be in awe of the information, the process had become part of my new identity. What I had initially thought of as paranormal had become normal.

The discovery of the 2013 Valentine's Day recording was a significant event, adding essential puzzle pieces to my life. I took my time, carefully inspecting all aspects of the message, attempting to decode it. I was shocked to learn my paralyzed vocal cord had prepared me to answer the angels' prophetic summons. I had become a voice by publishing *The Reluctant Messenger* in June 2018, three weeks after retirement.

I was curious and sought more information. How had I gone from psychologist to author in such a short period? I needed to know how it had happened, and to answer that question required me to review my past.

Delving into my life from five years before, I searched for clues. Shivers of knowing racked my body as a tiny spark of remembrance ignited. The last part tumbled into place, and I finally understood the genesis of my channeling. My ability to become a voice for the nonphysical had begun with yet another trip to Monroe Institute. I felt like one of J. R. R. Tolkien's hobbits as my adventures led me to another unexpected journey, there and back again, to where it had all begun, at Monroe Institute.

My trip to the institute in February 2013 had resulted in the miraculous healing of my speaking voice. Little did I know an equally significant event would occur five months later. While at a graduate-level program at Monroe, my spiritual voice was born.

In July 2013, I attended a program called Lifeline. Monroe Institute's website describes Lifeline as a "first-of-its-kind program that can empower you with the extraordinary ability to journey into the afterlife state and be of service to others."[1] The participants enter "specific states of awareness associated with the afterlife" and learn to "make contact with people who have passed over." At the program's end, the participants have the skillsets to make retrievals at will, independently assisting in future afterlife rescues.

I arrived on July 20. It was a warm Saturday afternoon when my connecting flight from Charlotte, North Carolina, landed in Charlottesville, Virginia. I disembarked and searched the lobby of this small airport for someone dressed in Monroe Institute clothing. Mike checked me off his list and said we would be waiting fifteen minutes or so for another incoming flight. Once everyone arrived, we loaded into the institute's van for the forty-minute ride to the campus.

Returning to Monroe Institute feels like a homecoming. I had planned this trip with Laurin, my friend from Appleton, Wisconsin. She had arrived earlier and had settled in the room we'd be sharing for the next six days. Our trainers were Kevin Turner and Scott Taylor. Kevin had extensive training in shamanism. Scott's

1 www.monroeinstitute.org

expertise was in near-death and shared-death experiences.

I nodded as the trainers told us to ask for information during the exercises. As a psychologist, I understood the importance of data collection to verify findings. Scott and Kevin also instructed us to search for people who had recently died; they were easier to contact. I think all the participants were a little apprehensive when we entered our booths for the first session.

A wave of anxiety washed over me as I listened to the voice on my headphones that guided us to search for newcomers. What if I couldn't do this? A few minutes passed, but nothing happened. I waited a little bit longer and still nothing.

I had attended several programs at Monroe, and over time I had learned to trust their methods. For reasons I cannot explain, I sat up and reached outside my meditation area and fumbled for my phone. Once I found it, I opened the voice memo program and tapped the record button.

I didn't think about asking for data; in fact, without having any conscious thought, I spoke a man's first and last names into the recorder. Next, I said, "Topeka, Kansas." The third piece of information I received was another proper noun. I don't know how I knew, but I understood this name was not a family name.

The voice on the audio exercise guided us to help our newcomers connect with friends and loved ones who had previously transitioned. I was operating in new territory, but it felt right to call my guides and angels to help usher this man to the other side.

When the exercise ended, almost on a whim, I opened my phone's web browser before joining the others to debrief our first session. In the back of my mind, I questioned the possibility of connecting with people who had passed and helping them transition. Although I respected the institute's research-based sound technology, I've learned to trust but verify.

I entered the man's first and last names, city and state, and almost as an afterthought, I added the word "obituary." Seconds later, my heart pounded, and I gasped as I looked at my phone's screen. I was staring at his online death notice.

My hands were shaking, and I had to take a few deep breaths to calm myself before I could read the information. Each line brought me closer to the outer fringes of my belief system. I felt as if I were on a mysterious hike between the worlds, like a tightrope walker, balancing on the thin edge between life and death, past and future.

The first two lines of the obituary verified several pieces of information I had received, including his first and last names and the city and state of his birth. We had been instructed to contact newcomers, and the death notice verified he had passed away exactly three months before, to the date. For some reason, this precision added significance to this already unforgettable event.

As I scrolled through the information on my phone, I realized what a beloved man he had been and how many lives he had touched with his passion for helping others. Midway through the article, another validation stunned me as a word seemed to jump off the screen in my direction.

Mystery solved. That other name I'd received that I knew was not a family name? It was the place of his employment, but the synchronicities didn't stop there. This much-loved man had been a psychologist; we shared the same profession. Although I had not received that information beforehand, it seemed the collective energy of being psychologists had brought us together. Like attracts like.

Throughout the week, I retrieved others whose information I also verified: first, middle, and last names, cities and states where they lived, and sometimes places of business. When I searched online, all were newcomers except one man who had transitioned one year ago from the day of his rescue.

After multiple exercises, my focus changed. I no longer

needed to collect personal data; I had nothing to prove because I knew the process was, indeed, genuine. Instead, I concentrated on assisting multiple spirits simultaneously. There were so many souls dwelling between Earth and the afterlife. After six days of intense practice, I left Monroe Institute as a changed person, and my belief in the process connecting us to nonphysical realms transformed into a known.

In retrospect, I came to understand what had happened. My Lifeline experience had cascaded through my well-established belief system like a giant tsunami, rearranging everything in its wake. I reached a tipping point, and everything I knew or thought I knew crumbled before me. Once this spiritual tidal wave passed, my life changed as knowns replaced my stripped-away, discarded beliefs.

It didn't happen all at once; I was initially oblivious to the significance Lifeline would have on me. I slept on, not knowing my life had changed, not knowing what had happened, not knowing how Lifeline had transformed me. But within two weeks, the first noticeable changes emerged as I began to channel messages from the unknown. As predicted, but not yet remembered, I had become *the voice of those who need to be heard* by chronicling those messages and publishing them in my first book, *The Reluctant Messenger*.

My metaphysical sleuthing had paid off. I had dug, probed, exposed, and examined my life from five years before, and I finally had the answer to *how* I had become a voice. It had been my Lifeline experience, and I had brought my new-found skills with me as I left the institute.

Once back home, the training wheels were off, and I was ready to go it alone. Unbeknownst to me, the institute's exercises had laid the foundation for my channeling abilities to surface—which they did two weeks later.

Not only had Lifeline prepared me to become a spokesperson for the nonphysical, but I also knew how to assist others with their final transitions. Several months later, when a friend was in the final stages of his Earth life, I was there to help.

A wave of uncertainty washed over me. Could I do this independently? Helping a friend was more personal than assisting strangers during Lifeline. I struggled with my doubts but only briefly. Verifying personal information during the program had authenticated the process, and I knew to assist with transitions was an actuality. I embraced the challenge to help with his sacred journey, and I was rewarded by witnessing his joyful reunion with the family who greeted him on the other side.

A couple of weeks after helping my friend enter the afterlife, the messengers spoke about the role of angels in this retrieval process:

January 4, 2014

Connecting Earth plane essence to the afterlife dimension requires assistance from the angel realm. This is the most appropriate energy system to aid humans who are ready to shed their physical bodies. The angelic energies combine with the retriever's energy field to form an interdimensional bridge. Once connected, the retriever can weave together the edges of both dimensions, thus allowing communication between the one passing and their friends or family in spirit.

When energy from humans combine with angels to help transition to the afterlife, the human becomes a Spirit Weaver. The Spirit Weaver stitches the two dimensions with an energy thread, not unlike that of a spider's web-diaphanous and frail appearing, yet powerful and able to withstand tremendous tension.

I'd had many messages about energy vibrations and frequencies, and over time my thinking had evolved. I now view most life events through the lens of energy. The angels had described themselves as a set of energies, so becoming an interdimensional bridge and weaving together frequency fields fit neatly within my frame of reference.

I realized how well my training at Lifeline had prepared me to accept this paradigm shift. Robert Monroe, Monroe Institute's founder, used research-based language to describe various states of consciousness, assigning numerical levels to them. Each focus level corresponded to specific brainwave frequency distributions associated with his patented sound technology called Hemi-Sync®.[2] While many might refer to the other side as heaven, he called it focus 27.

The impartiality of Monroe's vocabulary and the experiences at the institute made it easy to view all connections through different frequency vibrations. I realized energy is the common denominator in all communications, both physical and nonphysical.

The message changed, becoming more personal, explicitly addressing my recent assistance with my friend's final journey:

This one's last connection to us demonstrated the importance and power of this work. She had been instrumental in helping a loved one transition from their Earth plane existence.

As the angelic energies entered this one's field, she became aware of a connection with source. She was aware that she became a powerful, beloved angel, loved immeasurably by source.

Was I becoming an angel? I was surprised and confused, yet I accepted what they said. During retrievals, I use my energy to connect to the afterlife dimension. By combining my frequency

---

2 https://hemi-sync.com/learn/how-hemi-sync-works/

field with those I assisted, we become one unit, an interdimensional bridge. The more I thought about it, the less esoteric it sounded, and I found my definition of angels becoming more fluid as it changed with these new parameters.

I smiled as these thoughts entered my mind. I had learned so much from the angels and the other nonphysical agents. The message continued, describing how they had assisted during the retrieval:

We were able to enter her energy field. She felt welcomed by our energy, for she knew that she was home. On a certain level, she realized the connection, and it brought tears to her eyes. She was shown the magnificence of her source. She realized she was a potent and beloved spirit.

She was able to use this powerful connection to weave together the Points of Existence between this person's Earth plane essence and the essence of the other side. She used filaments of our energy to stitch the two realms together, so the loved one could connect clearly with spirits that had crossed over. He was able to see and communicate with family members who had already left the Earth plane.

At this point, most of the Earth plane essence had left his physical body, but not all. Any remaining fears dissipated when this person was able to connect with the spirits of family and friends. This person knew that they were waiting when he was ready to release his physical body.

As I heard the words of the messenger, a profound sense of peace came over me. I inhaled deeply, and in that meditative breath, I understood the impact Lifeline had on me. My most valuable lesson in life occurred during that six-day program at Monroe Institute: Lifeline had taught me physical death is a doorway to another chapter of continuing life. We do not die; our spirits, our souls remain. It was a sacred honor and a great privilege to assist someone on their final journey, but Lifeline had also given me a new skill—the ability to become a voice for the nonphysical.

Going back to Monroe had given me a new perspective. With this new viewpoint, my definition of angels continued to morph. I realized angels are not lofty winged creatures that fly among the clouds. They are high-vibrational energy beings who primarily inhabit nonphysical realms. Their energy signatures are different than ours because they exist much closer to the Creator.

In late March 2014, in response to my plea for protection from a stalker, the angels sent an energy that felt like a warm blanket of compassion, cradling me with eternal bliss. Every cell in my body quivered with these powerful vibrations, and I sobbed in response to this divine love that I knew was personalized for me.

Not only was I thankful for their help, but their messages revealed they had been guiding and protecting me throughout my life. They said the act of asking for assistance would summon them by igniting a field and lighting the path of connection. The next message arrived a week later with a slightly different twist:

April 8, 2014

We are now part of this one's system of awareness. We are in a position of guidance and protection, as well as serving as a source of information. We can share information with her, allowing it to flow into her awareness or upon request from her.

Angels assist when asked. I had always believed they needed these requests to avoid interfering with valuable Earth School lessons, so the last sentence of the message surprised me. Because they are now part of my system of awareness, it seemed invitations were no longer a requirement.

Although I knew asking for angelic help couldn't be a hard, fast rule, knowing my guidance system connected with divine assistance gave me a sigh of relief. Did this mean the angels would be more readily available? Like an upgrade to a computer's operating system, would things work the same, only better?

I know of people who live a charmed life where nothing seems to go wrong. Even when something seemingly negative happens, circumstances change to make it a positive event. Were they living with this angel hardware update? The message continued:

We are a subgroup of guidance located within the heart of the angelic energy system. When this one calls upon us, our Points of Existence moves directly into her heart space and radiates 360 degrees from there in a three-dimensional "globe-all" manner. Our globe of awareness encompasses and overlaps her energy field.

Calling upon us for assistance engages the overlapping effect and helps soften the edges of disruptive energy. Our quiet influence upon the human's energy field can light a favorable path as well as serve as a beacon for other seekers.

This is all one needs to do to call upon us. From that point on, we can guide the energy field and help soften energy patterns.

When unkind words are directed toward another human, the receiver's energy field becomes rough around the edges. When our energies are installed as part of the human's guidance system, we are able to smooth these edges to reduce negative emotional impact.

The angels continued, stating they altered my vibratory frequency as they integrated into my guidance system. The change resulted in a better energy match for my destined path. When my energy body vibrates at higher rates, I'm less likely to find myself in adverse situations. Positive energies enter my field of awareness. Things seem to go more smoothly, from fewer red traffic lights to better relationships.

These 2014 communications with the angels suggested we had, indeed, established a closer relationship. I knew they were here, guiding and helping. Without a doubt, they assisted in my day-to-day activities. Little did I know that assistance was about to intensify.

My recent dialogue with *Lighting the Void* podcast host Joe Rupe had brought me back to my 2014 messages with the angels, and Joe's conversation had reignited my relationship with these divine beings of light. Once I decided to write this book, the angels reappeared in my life, bringing waves of new communication that occasionally surprised me.

They sometimes led me down circuitous paths, revealing truth through symbols that mystified me. I eventually discovered the meaning behind these sometimes-enigmatic events, but there was always one constant: their loving energy.

It was time to put my words into action. As I gathered material for the book, I began to realize the importance of angels in my life. I searched my online documents and found multiple entries from my meditation and dream journals. One of the more impactful was the Valentine's Day message describing the reason my vocal cord was paralyzed, foretelling I would become a voice for the angels.

I pasted the Valentine's Day message in the manuscript that I had started a few weeks before. A smile lit my face when I realized this document would become another book. I glanced at my computer's clock. It was Wednesday morning, February 27, 2019.

My June 2018 retirement had changed the face of Monday mornings as I transitioned from full-time psychologist to part-time Nana and part-time author. My time constraints eased; no more 4:40 a.m. alarms shattering the stillness of a good night's sleep.

Although my alarm was on permanent hiatus, I still woke before sunrise. On this day, I had showered, dressed, and made a pour-over cup of Ethiopian coffee I had bought from Cassie. I was a big fan of my daughter's side business, Banyan & Bean Roasting Company. I glanced at my watch; just a little over three hours of writing time remained before switching to my role as Nana.

Shalane's half-day pre-kindergarten program three days a week worked well with my new life as a retiree. We had a structured routine. I'd pick her up at 1:00 and drive to her home. Next, we'd go through her backpack for items that might require her parents' attention. I'd open her lunch box, and she'd nibble on her remaining meal before picking a snack from the well-stocked pantry.

Shalane was approaching three years of age, and that meant her once-sacred afternoon naps were sporadic. With or without her afternoon snooze, we still had plenty of time to read and play before making the trek to the end of the block to meet her sister's school bus. Lorelai was always happy to see us after a full day at school.

The thoughts of my granddaughters had flashed into my mind when I glanced at the time. I needed to get back to writing, but my thoughts were interrupted again. I felt the familiar pull of a nearby messenger, so I opened my online journal and recorded the following:

February 27, 2019

When connecting to our realm, streams of energy are engaged. Because this one has made a conscious connection to us, a simple prayer, thought, or intention is enough to ignite the path. The thought, prayer, or intention sends a signal to our dimension, and we respond immediately.

We are ever watchful. Many times, humans discover life lessons through trial and error. Sometimes the more difficult training comes through the paths of failure, so we do not wish to interrupt the process, yet we are on the wayside, watching and waiting for the summons.

As these words spilled across my computer's monitor, I thought about the times that angels had protected and guided me. I understood the connection to them was through engaging streams of energy, but I wanted to know how and why.

Communication with the messengers was often subtle, and the connections frequently occurred as the result of engaging curiosity. By the act of pondering a question, answers arrived, cloaked in the silent fog of knowingness. It seemed my inquisitiveness had served, once more, as an unspoken invitation for answers. The angels guided me to study an older message. Once again, I needed to journey there and back again to understand the present. The older communication follows:

June 4, 2014

What this one does not yet realize is the reason for the connection to these various energy systems that have come into her existence. She was originally a part of each of these energy systems; they are all part of her collective source. This is why there is a connection, an attraction, to her. Her true essence connects these energy systems.

The human body is composed of the energy of stardust. This stardust energy is a combination of multiple energy systems that have transcended space and time. As this one continues to expand consciousness, she will become more aware of other energy systems from her source.

36

As I reexamined this older message, the references to stardust caught my attention. Humans composed of stardust? I was eager to research this, and, once again, I found myself in awe as my investigation supported the connection.

On National Geographic's website, Astrophysicist Karel Schrijver and his physician wife, Iris, validated the human-stardust link. They stated, "Everything we are and everything in the universe and on Earth originated from stardust, and it continually floats through us even today." Their book, *Living with the Stars*, describes the human body's connection to these celestial objects.[3]

As I explored the website, another uncanny correlation caught my attention. The messengers had reported of ancient roots and stardust energy that had *transcended space and time*. This account matched National Geographic's description of the origin of all parts of the human body from cosmic explosions billions of years ago.

This research answered my question as to why I had connected to many nonphysical energy systems. The 2014 message suggested ancient cosmological fragments of my past were part of me, and it was the stardust that had bound these long-ago bits to my current lifetime. It was our shared connection through stardust that generated the attraction, and these hidden aspects continued to summon my ancient homes.

Yet again, the messenger instructed me to search for answers in older communications. Perhaps this was a merging pattern of using the past to explain the present. After all, I had found a five-and-one-half-year-old recording that provided current answers about my medical miracle.

I couldn't help but wonder whether I had not been ready for the truth when it occurred years before, but now I am. Was this

3 www.nationalgeographic.com/news/2015/01/150128-big-bang-universe-supernova-astrophysics-health-space-ngbooktalk/

part of an intricate woven pattern of reality as the present picks up threads from the past to secure the foundation for the future?

I smiled as I realized I didn't know those answers, but I had long ago learned to trust that the truth would be forthcoming. I sat at my computer and added the 2019 message and its 2014 counterpart to my manuscript.

Writing this new book would be an exciting adventure, and I was eager to see what would unfold. I would return to writing tonight, but it was time to switch to my role as Nana and pick up Shalane from her pre-kindergarten class. I couldn't think of a better way to end my morning: communing with angels then playing with Shalane.

Two days later, I woke with a chill in the air; I jumped from bed to close the window. It was in the low sixties, pretty cool for March in South Florida, so I hopped in the shower to get warm. After I dressed and brewed a cup of hot coffee, I checked my email. Soon I would need to get ready to attend Friday's morning meditation at Goddess I Am.

This local metaphysical shop, owned by Beth Brown-Rinella, is filled with books, sage, crystals, jewelry, but it's more than just that. It's a mecca for those on a spiritual path, with services including meditations, massage, classes, psychic readings, and healing. Beth's Friday morning meditation has become an integral part of my June 2018 post-retirement routine.

I gathered my sweater, purse, journal, a couple of pens and off I went. I enjoy arriving early; it gives me a chance to tap into the energy of the room. During this pre-event interval, I often get a cosmic heads-up about the upcoming meditation.

As I sat in my chair with my journal in my lap, a familiar nudge told me to get ready to write. Something was different, though. I didn't recognize the energy; I immediately knew a new messenger had arrived.

March 1, 2019

Newness, freedom, rebirth. As a new month is upon you, oh, ye children of the Earth, the illusion of time creeps in like a morning fog. Its true nature resides within a dimension in which Earthlings must abide.

Not only was the energy different, so was the vocabulary. I was a bit surprised when I heard *oh, ye children of the Earth* and *Earthlings.* These were not typical words from my other nonphysical correspondents, and I was curious to hear more. The message continued:

Clock time. Calendar time. Seasonal time. When to sow. When to reap. When to rise. When to bed. But the dimensional spaces found within this construct called time have a basis in the multiverse. Patterns of energy underlie the concept, guiding the changes that are necessary for Earth life to occur and function within the density required for your existence.

We say to you to step deeper into time, to beyond the self-imposed limits set by the human mind. Use your intuition to release the chatter within your brain so that you may delve deeper into the true guidance that lies deep within that pool of true knowledge and wisdom. Know that you are loved. The light, truth, and wisdom that lies deep within your soul is yours. It is your birthright.

Receive these gifts that have always been yours. Open your heart to accept your birthright. Acceptance is the key.

Several minutes after the new messenger spoke, the meditation began, and Beth guided us to accept gifts from spirit that were inherently ours. The topic didn't surprise me; it corresponded with the message about knowing your birthright.

As the event came to a close and I gathered my belongings to leave, I thought about this new messenger. I'm always excited to meet a new emissary and see what further information they might share. I was eager to hear more.

I thought about the powerful words they shared. I realized each of us is born with eternal wisdom that resides within. Lessons seem to be part of the process allowing more in-depth looks into ourselves. Are life lessons the key to unmask our true nature as it brings inner wisdom to the forefront? It seemed so.

When we learn through experiences, there's an unburdening as we realize what works and what causes pain. As we traverse the seas of life, we release beliefs that no longer serve us. Our life lessons uncover truths from deep within, one layer at a time. This process illuminates the path of our birthright—divine guidance.

A couple of days later, another chill from my opened window woke me earlier than usual. I wrapped myself in a light blanket and sipped hot coffee on my balcony as I waited to greet the morning sun. The overnight low was in the mid-sixties, but soon it would be the perfect temperature for a nature hike.

The Gordon River Greenway is an eight-minute drive away and a perfect place to start this Sunday morning. I had just loaded my gear in the car when a messenger arrived. I opened my phone's voice memo app and tapped the record button.

As the messenger spoke, my perspective changed, and a different energy moved into my chest. Tears flooded my eyes and spilled down my face; I knew I was in the presence of angels. I recorded the following:

March 3, 2019

When a human connects to an energy system, this connection establishes a path. And like a path traversed in snow, the way is easy to follow for subsequent connections.

Thoughts are energy, and thoughts that combine with clear intention and a silenced mind are the conduits for connection. Just as plugging an electrical device into a wall outlet provides energy for the device to operate, setting an intention allows specific connections to energize. When humans connect with the higher vibratory frequencies of love, compassion, empathy, understanding, and gratitude, their surrounding energy emanates these characteristics.

As humans consciously connect with nonphysical energy systems, they become more deliberate in their choices. These higher vibrations attract more of the same. As they collect similar energy, the entire system begins to vibrate at a higher frequency. Some have called this enlightenment.

As the human essence becomes less encumbered, its tether to the Earth plane loosens. They experience subtler realms of existence, and they begin to sense energy shifts. Dreams become lucid and vivid as heart-based decisions begin to guide their lives. Prayer connects them to even higher vibrations, and like this one, they may find themselves receiving messages from nonphysical sources, including the angel realms. These energies permeate all humans just as stardust floats through humans today. Yet it is not the energies as much as the awareness of these energy shifts that change their lives.

Oh, ye children of the Earth, know that we are with you. Know that you are loved beyond measure. Know that we walk by your side, hoping you will feel the love that we have for you.

When I heard *Oh, ye children of the Earth*, this could only mean one thing: the new messenger had returned. With that realization, a vivid image formed in my mind, one I had known from bible stories I had read as a child.

In the bible book of Genesis, Jacob describes his dream of a ladder that connected heaven and Earth. The new messenger was showing me this structure, including ascending and descending angels. What did this mean?

Two days before, the angels said it was our birthright to know the wisdom and guidance from the spiritual realms. Did the vision of Jacob's ladder represent that birthright, a connection with higher vibrational beings? These connections empower us, bringing us closer to a state of enlightenment.

It wasn't just Jacob's ladder; there was a lot more to unpack from these recent messages. I couldn't help but smile when the new messenger referenced the human-stardust connection, mirroring the June 2014 message I had recently reviewed and researched. Did I need to go back to move forward?

I chuckled at that thought when I recalled the March 1 message to delve deeper into knowledge and wisdom by stepping beyond time constrictions. Was I overthinking this, letting my analytical mind override my intuitive nature? I knew more pieces would eventually fall into place. I had to remind myself to keep the energy flowing because being open often brought wisdom and answers.

Two communications in three days; this new messenger was persistent. Where would this lead? I didn't have long to find out. We met again three days later.

It was the first Monday of the month, and I rode with friends to the twice-monthly Crystal Bowl Meditation and Energy Healing at Church of Spiritual Light in Fort Myers, a church that had become my home away from home.

My thoughts drifted to my first visit in October 2015 to this interfaith, all-faith church led by Reverends Renee Bledsoe and Maribel Figueroa. It's a magical place for seekers to join together to celebrate divinity within themselves and others. After the hour-plus drive from Naples, I was ready to relax, but the messengers had a different plan.

We entered the church, signed in, and looked for a place to settle. The large crystal bowls sat in a semi-circle in the center of the room, surrounded by many blanketed cots. In thirty-minutes, the lights would dim in preparation for Yvette to play the bowls and the healing practitioners to begin.

I put my belongings on a cot and walked to the restroom at the back of the church. As I opened the bathroom door, I saw a picture of a wolf that was part of a large framed collage of various animals, icons, and other images. For some reason, I focused only on the wolf's nose. I wondered why.

Next, my attention drifted to a bottle of rosemary-scented hand soap, tucked behind rolls of paper towels on a shelf. I often receive cues about upcoming spiritual communications, so I wondered whether tonight's message might involve the sense of smell. As that thought entered my mind, I heard the word "alchemy," followed by a message about senses. I rushed back to my cot and pulled out my journal to jot down the following:

March 4, 2019

As you learn to fine-tune your senses, you shall tap into the divine nature of all that is. Allow this divine flow to transform you.

As you tap into your divine nature, the spirit and essence of those from the angel realm come forth. Hearts open, and with the opening of the heart, the energy flow throughout the body increases. As the flow increases, the cells become enlivened. They fill with divine energy.

With these words, the room transformed. The cots surrounding the crystal bowls in the center of the room morphed into lotus petals. On a level beneath the surface of conscious awareness, I understood this room-sized blossom was alive and filled with the divine energy of angels. The lotus blossom represented us, the participants, as we tapped into the sacred nature of the universe. The message continued:

Allow the energy vibrations to soften the edges of pain, soften the edges of mental discord. Allow for the balancing of energy for full healing to occur.

Intermittent lyrics from a Christian hymn, *Holy, Holy, Holy*, began to play in my mind. As I heard these lines, I somehow knew the blessed-trinity phrase held a nontraditional meaning for me. While the song played in the background, the message continued:

There is perfection, harmony, and a divine trinity. There is perfect health when the connection is divine.

The petals folded into the center of the meditation room, reminding me of a flower that closes at sunset. My vision panned back toward the ceiling, giving me an overhead view of the room. I looked down, expecting to see the bud of a lotus flower, yet an enormous red rosebud laid where the bowls had been.

A sense of awe came over me as I realized what I was seeing. I gained a new perspective, and I realized this was us—all of it. We had become the lotus petals; we had merged and transformed to create this bright red rosebud.

I noticed motion below. A stem formed at the base of the bud and began spiraling downward. My perspective followed the stalk as it traveled through the floor and deep into Earth's crust until it anchored itself around a crystal at the center of our marvelous planet.

My eyes returned to the nearly closed blossom in time to see golden flecks bubbling from its center. Two parallel wisps of fragrant sparkles meandered upward, and I realized these twin streams resembled the ladder from yesterday's meditation. Something deep within told me these wandering currents of energy were entering the angel realm.

I heard the words "Jacob's ladder" and, once again, I saw a replay of yesterday's vision with angels ascending and descending this sacred structure. Today's image, however, offered more details. Archangels entered first, followed by throngs of other angels. Unlike the up-and-down movement from the previous day, these angels only moved in one direction; I watched in awe as they descended into the room.

I was engulfed with a powerful energy of compassion as they entered this sacred church, and I sobbed when I realized they were there for us, the meditation participants. Tears streamed down my face as I scribbled in my journal, trying to document the detailed scenes that played in my mind's eye.

My eyes returned to the two golden streams of sparkles that had formed the ladder. I had an epiphany when I realized the significance of its shape—the double helix DNA strand. The DNA strand was Jacob's ladder, that divine instrument of connection between our realm and the angel realm, heaven.

Was that the blessed trinity from *Holy, Holy, Holy* I had heard? Could the trinity represent Earth, heaven, and DNA? I basked in the realization that we were the flower, that sacred flower connected to the angel realm by way of Jacob's ladder, our DNA.

Without warning, my conscious awareness faded. Within seconds I drifted into a peaceful oblivion that was deeper than sleep. Was this in response to the powerful angelic energy? Time slipped away, and I drifted within this peaceful abyss until something startled me awake. I looked around; I was standing in the middle of a snow-driven plain with teepees scattered in the distance.

I heard a noise behind me and turned in that direction. I was just feet away from a large white buffalo. His breath looked like plumes of steam from a locomotive as he pawed the snow-covered ground in search of something to graze.

I blinked to refocus. What I saw couldn't be right. I knew I was at Church of Spiritual Light, but a cold winter's wind blew through my hair, and my bare feet felt the numbness of impending frostbite. An angel spoke, explaining I had traveled back in time. The message continued:

This is divine healing. As you open your awareness to the divinity from the angels who surround you, you can step back into time and heal the wounds of the past. Allow, allow, simply allow and accept the Creator's divine healing as gifted by the Angel of Grace.

Two days before, this new angelic messenger had instructed me to step deeper into time, and here I was, standing in a snowy field surrounded by a white buffalo and teepees with the explanation I had traveled back in time.

These heavenly forces guided me like a river's undercurrent that flows just below the surface of awareness. They were leading me somewhere or to something, and I felt myself slip further down the rabbit hole as the larger picture began to develop.

My mind flashed back to August 28, 2013, the date of my first contact with a messenger. The initial communique that described a flower as a flow-er of energy was the first puzzle piece. I smiled at the similarities to this day's meditation. The double-helix of Jacob's ladder that connected Earth to heaven had emerged from the rosebud—definitely a flow-er of energy.

Another clue was the similarities between today's meditation and my first visit to Church of Spiritual Light in October 2015: energy, healing, multitudes of angels, and even a white buffalo.

My spiritual journey flashed before my eyes. I realized this déjà vu moment had led me back to the beginning. This meditation had begun with the word "alchemy," that magical process of transformation and creation. It had, indeed, ended that way as angels descended through the double-helical of Jacob's ladder, our DNA.

DNA is our genetic code that makes you, you. It makes me, me. Every cell in our bodies has this molecule, and it is present in all forms of life on Earth. As I thought of these connections, I realized science and spirituality were not mutually exclusive. There is an ever-increasing knowledge of how they work hand-in-hand, explaining the unexplainable, leading the way for better choices for humanity.

These last few messages shined a light on the powerful undercurrent running through my life—angels. In a recording that had remained hidden for over five years, the angels explained everything. I learned why I had lost my voice and what I needed to do once I healed. And their hidden, prophesied communique of my miraculous healing had surfaced only when I was ready to comprehend the significance of these events.

These past few meditations had ushered new awareness into my life. It was time for me to acknowledge this and allow the interdimensional undertow of the angel realm to carry me back to the beginning—my beginning.

My consciousness explorations had brought me there and back again. I recalled the words of T. S. Eliot, "We shall not cease from exploration, and the end of all our exploring will be to arrive where we started and know the place for the first time."

I had come full circle—there and back again—and now I was ready to rediscover my world through the eyes of the angels.

CHAPTER 4: LIFE FORCE WEAVERS

Does your life flash before your eyes when you die? According to my angelic friends, the answer is a resounding yes. Although I was not surprised by that reply, the reasons for the life review astounded me.

My Lifeline adventure at Monroe Institute and my most recent journeys into the unknown had brought the awareness of angels back into my life. I knew they were a collection of energies tasked with guiding and protecting me. The angels stated they had accompanied me when I entered the world, and they would do so during my final transition.

Recent interactions with them made me curious whether they could provide answers to some of the time-honored questions about the universe: Why am I here? What is the purpose of life? Is Earth simply a learning experience to help us become more spiritually aware or enlightened? Are we fully conscious in the afterlife?

As I pondered these issues, I remembered a messenger had previously spoken about the life review that occurs as part of our final transitions. Would these older entries provide answers? I searched my online journal and found a series of messages beginning late summer 2014.

Little did I know this trip down memory lane would weave

its existence into the present, and in doing so, would benchmark essential aspects of my awakening. These cosmic breadcrumbs from the past connected me with a vaster consciousness, one that is always in union with the angelic realm. I invite you to accompany me on this journey as the past weaves with the present in a mystical courtship of consciousness to provide age-old answers about life.

I glanced at the first 2014 journal entry. Reviewing my anecdotal notes associated with the message catapulted me back to that day. It was one year after I had attended Lifeline at Monroe Institute. The school year had just begun, and I struggled to adjust to the 4:40 a.m. alarm. I dragged myself into the shower, dressed, and ambled toward the elevator in my condominium. Although I usually take the stairs, I wasn't alert and didn't want to trip as I navigated the ten flights to the garage.

I exited the elevator and walked the short distance to my car. As I tossed my belongings in the passenger's seat and started the engine, a brief vision of the human body flashed into my awareness. I turned on my phone's recorder to describe the images from my mind's eye.

The figure was unlike any human body I had seen. The skin was completely transparent and, within its frame, floated different-sized translucent bubbles. An almost imperceptible shimmering cord weaved its way through the form, threading the bubbles together.

The connecting filament began to unravel, causing the bubbles to drift apart. Within seconds, these iridescent spheres floated away, and the matrix that had defined the person's shape was no longer there. The body had disappeared. The messengers explained my vision:

August 15, 2014

When humans drop their physical forms to transition, the

"glue" that holds their energy body begins to dissipate, allowing these bubbles to go forth, away from the physical body. This is why humans have life reviews. Memories of life are stored in these bubbles, but they are more than just memories. Because this is an energy connection, it is not limited to the five physical senses.

As the human transitions, the nonphysical self begins to take over, but this, too, is a transition as it moves toward its true nature. As the glue of life dissolves, the nonphysical being can study all aspects of their Earth plane existence through these energy bubbles.

The human reviews the Earth plane life as these bubbles of memory disengage from the physical body. But it is much more than a simple observation, for these energy packets can be experienced with a fuller set of senses. The human can see, hear, taste, smell, and touch any or all aspects within the memory bubbles. They not only re-experience the event with all emotions still intact, but they can relive it through the senses of others who might be part of that memory, even if only tangential.

The review offers a complete recapitulation of life events with exquisite detail not available during their existence on the Earth plane.

Releasing memory bubbles during the final transition was a new concept for me, and never did I expect to find corroborating evidence almost five years later. This thread from the past emerged in April 2019, when I purchased a series of Hemi-Sync® CDs that described what the messengers had reported.

Hemi-Sync® is a sound-based technology based on audio patterns using binaural beats. Founder Robert Monroe used multi-layered patterns of sound frequencies that guide the listener to various brain stages ranging from sleep to deep relaxation to expanded awareness and even other extraordinary states of consciousness.[4]

The *Into the Light: Near-Death Experience Meditations* CD contains four guided exercises created by Scott Taylor, an Near-Death Experience (NDE) researcher and speaker.[5] Dr. Taylor based his CD on the analysis of more than 6,000 case studies of NDEs.

Scott had recently become president and executive director of Monroe Institute, a place I loved, not only because of its outstanding residential programs, but this was where my miraculous healing had occurred in February 2013. Although Scott now oversees one of the world's foremost institutes dedicated to the study of human consciousness, I remember him as my Monroe Institute trainer during Lifeline in July 2013, five months after the miraculous recovery of my paralyzed vocal cord. This residential program changed my life, opening doors to a transformation that heralded my spiritual awakening.

Feelings of déjà vu washed over me as I listened to Dr. Taylor as he guided an exercise called *Life Review*. He spoke of glowing balls of energy that could transport the listener to important past memories to relive. Just as the messengers had indicated, the review included emotions and physical senses of others within the memory. Dr. Taylor reported consciousness exists in multiple places simultaneously: you as yourself, the observer, the other participants in the scene, and from an all-knowing, all-seeing omniscient perspective.

A sense of awe and wonder filled me as I listened to the CD and its uncanny similarity to the 2014 message. Tapping into these orbs of memory expands you into a higher state of consciousness that surpasses the normal waking state. This expansion allows a

---

4 https://hemi-sync.com/learn/how-hemi-sync-works/

5 https://hemi-sync.com/product/into-the-light-near-death-meditations-album/

glimpse into the ripple effect of your actions. An event you may have thought of as inconsequential might have life-altering effects on others. This process is such a fantastic tool to discover how your actions impact others. The message continued, revealing more details:

> *Just as various devas and elementals help in the plant realm, there are systems of energy that assist humans on a molecular level. These entities are the ones responsible, in part, for the functioning of organs in the human body.*
>
> *They are similar to Spirit Weavers who stitch dimensional spaces together, but these operate on a much smaller scale. They are Life Force Weavers, and they act as glue as they weave together the energy aspects of an individual. The Life Force Weavers hold together vital energy, making it whole and complete. These are part of the final touches in defining the entity as living. The Life Force Weavers embody life.*
>
> *There is an ungluing, an unraveling, as the physical body transitions to the next dimension. As this transition occurs, their woven lifetime events begin to loosen and unravel. These Life Force Weavers gently leave the space of the human to which they were assigned; they go forth to other duties.*
>
> *The unraveling frees the memory bubbles. They become loose and are no longer associated with the life the human had experienced. As they relinquish themselves from the physical body, they trigger the energy reaction that is called a life review.*

Life Force Weavers are the adhesive that keeps the memory orbs together. Their presence defines life. Dr. Taylor's research verified the information from my 2014 message and vision, but these additional details piqued my interest, and I craved more knowledge.

A week after this message, my understanding expanded as I learned Life Force Weavers, or perhaps their cosmological counterparts, exist on celestial levels:

August 21, 2014

There is no such thing as empty space for within the space that humans perceive as empty are energy frequencies, vibrations, and patterns. This is much like the Life Force Weavers that are found within the human body—a microcosm of the macrocosm. These energy patterns of so-called "empty space," function to keep the various celestial bodies in alignment and harmonic resonance with each other.

Whether they functioned on cosmic or individual levels, these entities operated in what appears to our limited physical senses as empty. Were there other connections? I didn't have long to find out.

A week later, amid multiple other-worldly communications, the messengers resumed their discussion about Life Force Weavers. It was early Sunday morning, and I hadn't yet made it out of bed. I used my Saturdays and Sundays to recover from the previous days and to gain needed energy for the upcoming workweek.

While in a state between dreaming and waking, I saw a woman who appeared to be praying or meditating. While sitting in silence, the luminous energy field outlining her body began moving. This shimmering shape wiggled free, and the edges stretched as it loosened and drifted away.

My inner vision shifted to a pair of cupped hands in front of my face. From an observer's perspective, I realized these were my hands, and they held a pile of minuscule sparkling residue that twinkled and glimmered as if alive. I intuitively knew it was stardust.

The me in the vision gently blew into my cupped hands, propelling the material upward. It floated in the air, moving in unison like a flock of birds soaring on air currents. As I marveled at the sight, I understood the connection. The body of stardust represented the radiant energy field of the woman I had observed; it was her life force energy.

Life Force Weavers unravel and retreat from the physical body upon death, but they stretch during some circumstances. This elongation allows the life-force particles to operate outside our physical bodies during states of expanded awareness such as meditation, prayer, or out-of-body explorations. Although stretched, the constant connection to the body's energy field is maintained.

August 28, 2014

The Life Force Weavers dance in the background of creation, giving meaning and purpose, giving life. To see them in action is, indeed, a beautiful sight.

We have spoken of the Life Force Weavers in the human body. At the time of transition when the physical body is no longer needed, Life Force Weavers leave, thus allowing the various energy particles and systems (containing expanded memories, thoughts, and action) to loosen.

With the loosening of the multiple energy bubbles which were once contained within the human's energy field, the human experiences the life review as they perceive these bubbles drifting away from the physical body. The life review is a result of the loosening bubbles of energy. The bubbles must disassociate from the physical body for the spirit or essence of the human to be able to return home to the Creator.

With the connection to meditation from a visual perspective, the process appears to be similar, yet it is not. The Life Force

Weavers stretch, but they do not unravel. As this interweaving cord lengthens, it becomes more luminescent. Many seekers have referred to this as the silver cord or the silver thread.

When the physical body drops away in what humans refer to as death, the Life Force Weavers leave the human's energy body, carrying with it all vital energy, that energy which is responsible for the physical body to consider itself to be alive.

During meditation, the vibrational frequencies of Life Force Weavers change as a direct result of the meditation or prayer and the intent of the human, thus allowing for stretching and subsequent activation of what humans refer to as the silver cord to stretch beyond its dormant state. From a visual perspective, it is not just one silver thread, but millions of luminous fibers connected to each energy bubble, essence, or packet which reaches toward Creator source.

The Life Force Weavers' luminous fibers stretch during meditation or prayer caused by a change of energy frequency, thus allowing extension of awareness from the human's normal energy field. These vibrational frequencies change in response to the energy of intent to meditate.

Life Force Weavers are the silver cord? I was fascinated by the information and curious to learn more. Perhaps this inquisitiveness paved the way for more learning, this time while I was asleep.

I went to bed that night and had a dream so vivid it felt like an out-of-body experience. I drove with friends to a deeply wooded forest to spend the day hiking and exploring a mountainous area that I somehow knew was in a different dimensional space.

In the dream, I found myself looking up from the base of a steep, rocky slope, and I knew I needed help to get to the top. I grabbed an exposed tree root that jutted from the rocky hillside. Pulling on it gave me enough leverage to ascend this challenging incline, but in doing so, part of it snapped off in my hand.

When I made it to the top, I was winded and a little sore. I glanced at my hand when I realized I was still holding the root. A glimmer of light radiated from its broken end. I shook the root, emptying its contents in my cupped hand, and I smiled as hundreds of small crystals spilled into my open palm.

When I woke and recorded the experience, I was amazed at the detail I remembered. I tried to make sense of it all. I appreciated the dream, and on some level, I knew it was significant. I wanted to comprehend it and for these images to shed meaning on the mystery that had become my life. I longed for the dream to reveal the truth that I've found often lives just beneath the surface of awareness. It didn't take long for the messengers to offer an interpretation:

August 29, 2014

Beginning with the dream last night, we are giving information about Life Force Energy and the Life Force Weavers. Life Force Energy is the larger system that oversees living energy fields. It contains everything vital for humans to experience life. It gives life force to anything alive, not just humans.

I thought of the crystals inside the hollow root in my dream. Did they represent the Life Force Energy? Was this what I had seen in the vision of the meditating woman? The message continued:

It is the Life Force Weavers, a subset of the Life Force Energy, which keeps the human's energy body intact. It literally weaves energy packets or bubbles together while the human's physical body is alive. It keeps things in place until the physical body is ready to drop away and make its final transition.

At times, a human may make a slow transition, and the

unweaving is gradual. When this occurs, humans report seeing others who have crossed over before them. They may see angels, for example, because the bubbles of their energy field have drifted from their physical bodies and into other dimensions.

In the case of coma, humans exist within an interdimensional space. The Life Force Energy has not left them, but the Life Force Weavers have not kept the tension taut. Therefore, there is a drifting of their energy field into other dimensions but not yet a complete unweaving.

Although this was new information to me, it seemed logical to have an overarching Life Force Energy that would guide the Life Force Weavers. The description of the stretching of the Life Force Weavers during the transitory state of coma was also a reasonable conclusion. The message continued:

When cells unite in utero to develop into a living being, it begins with a single cell, multiplying quickly. As the fetus develops, Life Force Energy and Life Force Weavers enter the small body yet maintain connection to the Creator source. Upon birth, this connection allows the infant to communicate with spirits in other dimensions.

I've observed newborns as they scan their world with newly gained vision. They look at their environment, appearing to perceive more than what our eyes are capable of seeing. Reviewing these 2014 messages also offered me a new perspective as well as a nostalgic trip down memory lane. Yet, something felt different.

In the five years since these 2014 messages, my inner eyes had opened. I had fallen into a rhythm of life that included trusting the wisdom of the words from the messengers. Validations, such as Scott Taylor's research of Near-Death Experiences, had confirmed many truths from the messengers.

I realized as I stepped further into the outer fringes of what had once been my limited belief system, more information flowed. In keeping with this line of thought, as the new perspective of these older messages wove into my current life, a new message arrived in apparent response about newborns' connections to the spiritual realm.

April 7, 2019

When human infants are born, a subgroup from their angelic transition team remains while the newborns accommodate to life inside a physical body. This same transition team will accompany this soul's true essence when the physical body is no longer operational — what humans refer to as death.

Before entering a human body, the spirit, the soul, the essence is expansive because it operated in the unified nonphysical world where it was unencumbered. As a soul transitions to become part of the human experience, it must sever its ties to the nonphysical and prepare to enter the restrictive world of form.

This is not an easy task, and it takes a concerted effort from our realm for them to cross the dimensional barrier. The purpose of this barrier is to reduce the energy load of the incoming spirit, for the fully charged nonphysical energy would overload human circuits, rendering them useless.

Although spiritual transition teams were a new concept for me, it not only seemed a reasonable assumption but a comfortable one. My ever-increasing knowledge of energy vibrations and frequencies gave credence to the theory that the incoming soul would be too strong and expansive to enter a physical body without causing damage.

When I experience visions, I often find myself in scenes where my physical senses operate more fully than in my normal waking state. I can only assume these expansive states of consciousness are glimpses into my true nature. If so, I can understand the challenges associated with compressing these powerful frequencies in a dense physical body. The message continued:

An aspect of the interdimensional barrier, the veil of forgetfulness, wipes the memory clean. Passing through the veil allows the soul to enter its human existence, anew, refreshed, a tabula rasa.

Hearing about a veil of forgetfulness brought me to a new level of understanding. If our experiences on Earth are for learning, removing prior knowledge would be necessary to allow a fresh start.

As we become more enlightened, the veil thins, and our higher selves slip into our awareness. These are parts that couldn't accompany us during our incarnations on Earth. They are aspects of our true essence.

When we increase our awareness, we begin to recognize subtle cues around us. We continuously gather these breadcrumbs, but we may not realize it at the time. One day, we reach a tipping point, and we no longer feel isolated. We know we are part of all that is as once-hidden events come into view. Perhaps this defines being psychic. The message continued:

During the mother's pregnancy, the soul travels back and forth between the nonphysical and the physical worlds. If the nonphysical can adjust to the constrictions of form within the human physiology, it gradually spends more time there.

Transition teams from our realm oversee much of this process. When compatibility matching is complete, a subset of the transition team remains with the soul until after birth. Newborn infants can see and communicate with this team.

Soon, however, the newborn team retreats to the nonphysical, traversing back through the barrier of the veil of forgetfulness, and the last vestiges of memory are wiped from the infant.

Once the newborn team returns to the nonphysical, the active role of the angels will shift to a protective state. We are always around, but not as readily visible as before the completion of the nonphysical to physical transition.

Many young humans are still able to communicate with us, for it had not been that long since they were part of the unmanifested world of the nonphysical. As humans grow and survive in the dense Earth plane energies, the veil of forgetfulness appears to strengthen, and it takes concerted effort to penetrate these subtle interdimensional barriers.

The more I learned from the angelic messengers, the more in awe I felt. I hoped I could use this information to step beyond my frail human limitations and make my life a spiritual expression of my true self.

I found myself drawn to this grand plan that orchestrated our lives on Earth. Life Force Weavers? Transition teams? A veil of forgetfulness to allow a fresh start? I felt a profound sense of gratitude as I realized the wisdom and intelligence of this brilliant design.

I felt a nudge to return to the 2014 messages. I opened my online journal and searched for more information about Life Force Weavers. I found several entries from November and December.

In November 2014, I had participated in an online meditation facilitated by Deepak Chopra and Oprah Winfrey. In the introduction, Dr. Chopra spoke of the intelligence of energy that was associated with the law of attraction. These words made sense to me, but they also piqued my interest. How did that work? I decided to ask the messengers.

November 6, 2014

We say that this intelligence is due to the Life Force Weavers. They are the vital energy, the vibration of aliveness that allows for what he [Deepak Chopra] calls intelligence of the energy of the law of attraction. Life Force Weavers thread their way through the energy system of the body, giving it life, thus making it vital.

Once the Life Force Weavers are part of the physical body, the humans interpret their bodies as separate from the rest of the universe. We know that this is not true, but most humans perceive themselves as individuals, as distinct and separate.

The vibrational frequency of the Life Force Weavers is universal and not just found within human life. These vital frequencies operate within what humans refer to as the law of attraction. It is essential to let go and allow life to move through you. Once humans realize they are not separate, they will enable their vibratory frequencies to pull them to their future, much like the pull of magnets on metal objects.

Allowing engages the activity of the Life Force Weavers operating within the framework of the law of attraction. This is how attraction works. It is a natural attraction that opens channels for more of the same.

When humans allow guidance, they are attracted to and then led down a path that is for their higher good, for this guidance is divine. It is from our realm. There are some of us whose sole purpose is to guide and guard humans. The path may not always be smooth; there may be bumps in the road, but those are the catalysts for change in a direction for the better, higher vibratory state.

It is not difficult for humans to engage the energy of their guidance system. Know that this is the connection to us.

Humans must understand there is not always a direct correlation between hard work and success without guidance. Allowing divine guidance within will result in more productive outcomes. Guidance strives for a vibratory match with the human heart.

The law of attraction is to be trusted. The Life Force Weavers within this law actively engage intentions, so be mindful of your thoughts, for the law of attraction is a basic rule of the universe, just as gravity is a basic rule on the Earth plane.

As with magnets, if you let go of the resistance, there will be a natural flow of energy, whether it be an item, an event, or an outcome.

With these words, an image formed in my mind of a fist-sized magnet attached to a metal object. In the vision, I pulled the magnet several inches from its source then released it. The magnet snapped back to its original position with such speed that it appeared as a blur. Releasing my resistance allowed the magnet's return to its source. The message continued:

Engaging the brain instead of the heart often results in rerouting Life Force Weavers away from the initial desire. Engaging the mind instead of the heart can cause resistance where the human's energy field is no longer allowing and flowing in the direction of the initial desire.

My attention returned to the vision. Again, I pulled the powerful magnet away, but this time I didn't release it. Instead, I lessened my resistance, allowing my arm and hand to gradually move toward the magnet's original source. The closer it got, the more resistance I felt, and I had to maintain constant and ever-increasing vigilance to prevent the magnet from jettisoning away. Stopping the natural rhythm of allowing the magnet to reconnect to its source resulted in friction, and it required constant resistance from me. The messenger continued where my vision ended:

As humans resist the flow of nature, the result is dis-comfort or dis-ease. This resistance causes an imbalance as the innate energies of the Life Force Weavers are blocked to pursue alternatives. The natural flow becomes disrupted as competing energies attempt to lure the energy away from its natural flow to source. This resistance can manifest in the human body as stress, upset, and disease.

The law of attraction operates by a magnetic pull between intention and action; therefore, by relinquishing resistance, the natural flow of energy returns to the item, event, or outcome of the intention.

The words brought me back to the images of the magnets. The natural flow of the separated magnet is toward the source, much like the action of following divine guidance. When we doubt our desires, the brain short circuits the natural rhythm and reroutes the energy like a self-correcting GPS. The law of attraction, by way of the Life Force Weavers, dictates a change as the initial intention veers off course toward the newly created destination of doubt or uncertainty.

A third magnet scenario played in my mind. I pulled the magnet away and released it, but it did not return to its source. Instead, it moved to another metal object, one that was closer.

The law of attraction is simply that—a law. With exact precision, it operates to bring similar frequencies together. Unless we want the paths to our goals to meander and swerve, we need to focus on guidance from the heart. Maintaining a consistent vibrational match between our hearts and intentions establishes a direct line toward our goals. But how can we keep this level of steadfastness in our desires and intentions?

The three visions of magnets crystalized my understanding of the law of attraction and the power of intention. The natural energy flow is toward the vibrational match, not necessarily its original source. The message continued:

Life Force Weavers exist in anything vital or living, including the law of attraction. It is easier for humans to perceive people, animals, plants, and even minerals as being alive. Yet, they often do not realize that the energy frequency of the Life Force Weavers exists in subtler areas.

There are basic universal laws of energy that are the foundations of existence. One such rule, of course, is what humans refer to as the law of attraction. What makes this a universal law is that it operates consistently and in a never-ending pattern. It is always there, much like the law of gravity, but most humans have difficulty understanding this. We are pleased to see some humans are beginning to acknowledge this fundamental law of the universe.

Everything is energy. Let us repeat. Everything is energy. Life Force Weavers are part of that energy system, making it intelligent energy. Let us give an example. When humans desire a specific item, event, or outcome, all possible things, occurrences, or outcomes exist within the energy field. Once the desire for a particular item, event, or issue is made known via a thought or intention, then the universal field of energy begins to blend to manifest the human's specific desire.

There is no work involved. It is a matter of physics. A magnet does not "work" to attract an item. Once something is within its energy field, the magnet draws it near. The surrounding field does the work. Like attracts like. The energy frequency of the desire travels into the ethers, and the universe responds with a similar vibrational pattern. Easy. Simple, no magic involved, just simple physics.

When the human puts forth the energy pattern of desire for the specific item, event, or outcome, the Life Force Weavers match the attraction to the energy field, pulling those vibrational frequencies within the human's reach.

It is a straight-forward process, but sometimes the vibrational frequencies of the desire are altered, which causes the Life Force Weavers to move toward the new attraction. Negative thinking often sabotages the human's initial desire. The frequency of "lack" enters, which then reroutes the Life Force Weavers to match the energy frequency of lack of the specific item, event, or outcome.

The key is awareness that the law of attraction is a universal energetic law. It is an active, dynamic, vital law due to the action of the Life Force Weavers. Have respect for it, and you will flourish.

Introducing the connection between Life Force Weavers and the law of attraction had expanded my understanding of their functionality. Processing my new knowledge had opened the door for more information, because five days later, I had received the following:

November 11, 2014

The seven primary chakras in the human body represent energy centers, the powerhouses of the body. The Life Force Weavers enter the body and spiral from the base chakra up through the crown chakra, weaving in and out in a vertical, serpentine pattern.

As they reach each chakra, a set breaks off from the primary Life Force Weavers and moves horizontally in the same weaving pattern that eventually forms a matrix around the human body. This matrix vitalizes the body and makes it alive.

A vision accompanied these words, and I saw the Life Force Weavers moving through the human body as described. Once they branched off at each major chakra, the weaving pattern continued, splitting again and again until an intricate matrix covered the figure. The message continued:

When it is time for the physical body to drop away, the Life Force Weavers begin to loosen their hold on the physical matrix before the final exit. This unweaving process allows for the energy that was associated with the human's existence to slough away. Because everything is energy, including thoughts and memories, the human experiences a life review.

I had learned this information before, but this time a vision accompanied the message. I saw an intricate pattern of memory bubbles that rose to the surface to be released. They were different sizes and translucent colors. Some spiraled upward in clusters while others remained singular. The message continued:

The life review serves more than one purpose. There is an emotional release as the human reviews life events from multiple perspectives. There is now a better understanding of the events, for their essence is no longer connected with the physical body — it has begun to reconnect with powerful source energy.

There is a voluntary life review called recapitulation. It does not occur as a result of the Life Force Weavers leaving the body as what happens upon physical death. The human can bring forth into awareness events they need to review. With a different perspective, these events take on different meanings than before.

If there is negative emotion associated with the event, the human can now release that negative energy back into the universe and no longer carry it. It is similar to forcing a splinter out of your skin that has been infected and is festering. It takes a concerted effort and perhaps some pain or uncomfortable feelings. However, when the fragment is released, the healing begins.

Life Force Weavers work with the intention of the human, and they can release the emotional hold that events have upon them. It unencumbers the energy surrounding the physical body, enabling the human to be free from energy ties that bind them to the physical world. It allows for the thinning of the veil.

I entered the information from these 2014 messages into the book draft, but I felt the need to put this chapter aside until I could complete further research. The recapitulation process was similar to Dr. Scott Taylor's *Life Review* exercise on his *Into the Light: Near-Death Experience Meditations* CD; I had to learn more.

I searched online to gain a better understanding and found an interesting story. Shaman Link's website has an article written by Lauren Torres entitled *Recapitulation, Reclaiming Your Energy*. Torres described recapitulation as a means to release personal energy back into the universe.[6]

Torres asserts this is an ancient shamanic process that allows the person to reclaim energy. Strong emotional feelings associated with past events and interactions indicate a continual association with them. The more energy connected to the past means less personal power for current use. Recapitulation releases the past, resulting in fresh energy to help you move forward. Your history no longer dictates the future; the past no longer drains or controls you.

---

6 www.shamanlinks.net/blog/recapitulation-reclaiming-your-energy

I have learned many lessons from the angels, but this one provided another tool in my consciousness-awareness toolbox. Getting a jump-start on the life review through voluntary recapitulation, frees me from energy-consuming memories, making room for more adventures to arise. Learning to recapture vital energy through released memories offered a new perspective. I only hoped my new outlook would serve me well and make me worthy as an ordinary intermediator of extraordinary messages.

Tracing foundations of recapitulation to ancient shamanism fascinated me, but adding Life Force Weavers to this voluntary life review created a delightful element that stirred my curiosity. I had already learned the energy connection of Life Force Weavers defined life within our physical bodies. The logical definition of death, therefore, must be the absence of the Life Force Weavers.

Were they the linchpins between life and death? Is their exit the last step in our final transition? As if on cue, I felt an urging from the messengers for another search. I laughed out loud when I realized my research detour had returned me to where I had begun—back to my messages journal. I opened it again and searched for yet another marker from memory lane and found the following:

December 12, 2014

There is no such thing as death. "Death" is a human term. Death is simply a door that one must pass through when you have been in the physical body. When the physical body wears out and is no longer functional, it becomes time for it to drop away and allow the spirit or soul to soar.

Death is stepping into another dimension. If those of you could experience what you refer to as death, and then remember that event, there would be no fear. It is no different than walking from one room of your house to another, and communication is still possible. There is nothing to fear.

As I reviewed these first few paragraphs in my online journal, I recalled the 6,000 NDE case studies Dr. Scott Taylor had analyzed, and I wanted more information. I opened my laptop's browser and began searching. I landed on the International Association for Near Death Studies (IANDS) homepage.[7]

The research revealed the majority of near-death experiencers describe being at peace and floating in a sense of total wellbeing during their transcendent events. I've had several conversations with people who expressed their near-death experiences as being so blissful that they did not want to return to their physical bodies.

This information was hand in glove with the messenger's words, indicating fear of death is strictly from a human point of view. The transition we call death is peaceful. I turned my attention to the rest of the message:

Reincarnation is just another path for the true essence, spirit, or soul to live in yet another physical body with another opportunity for growth. When the spirit or soul is free from the physical, the energy reconfigures to allow a new life when the spirit is ready to return to a physical body. The essence of the person is the same, but there is a melding and meshing of energy based on previous life experiences.

Everything is energy. Lessons and choices in the Earth plane carry a specific energy signature. Hobbies, families, friends, all influence the energy field of the human. All of these energies dissipate when the physical body drops away.

I loved revisiting these older messages; they often brought new insights. In the past, I might not have embraced

---

7 https://iands.org/ndes/about-ndes.html

reincarnation, but visiting this topic more than five years later offered a different perspective. It now makes sense to me. I had learned to view the world through the lens of energy, and having my soul enter another physical body in a different lifetime fit in that paradigm of life and my ever-evolving belief system. The message continued:

We have already shared with this one about the life review and how the life review not only shares lessons but allows the letting go of all of the energies held during that lifetime. The collection of life powers merge with the soul to help reconfigure the energy in preparation for another incarnation.

I was curious about the reference to additional life review messages, and at the same time, I wondered how much further I would travel down this rabbit hole. I entered "life review" in the search bar and found the entry. It was twelve months before the 2014 message I had just reviewed:

December 19, 2013

In the past, this one dreamed about what is referred to as the life review when humans cross over. Go back and review that lesson, for now, it can be viewed with a different light.

I smiled and shook my head when I realized this was a request for yet another review of material. It seemed this rabbit hole was never-ending. I changed gears and searched my dream journal.

Dreams have fascinated me since childhood, and I began recording them in a word document in the late 1990s. By April 2019, my dream journal had reached over 230,000 words, so I much appreciated the built-in search feature. When I typed "life review," an entry from 2002 filled my computer's screen.

Although the dream had occurred many years before, I remembered its message: "July 6, 2002: Saturday morning. I woke early, then went back to sleep and had this dream: I was in heaven, and someone showed me how it worked. Everyone had to go through the life review because it was a way of releasing all of the final Earth energies. The life review is not just a learning tool. It physically prepares you to be a being of light. Once the life review is completed, you are able to walk through the Infinite Light of God."

Reviewing the 2002 entry in 2019, offered me a different perspective, and I paused to think. At the time of the dream, I realized the vocabulary was not my typical phraseology, but I had not given that much thought until now.

A lot had happened since the 2002 dream, including my association with the messengers. When I read the phrase "Infinite Light of God," cold chills covered my body, and I couldn't help but wonder if the messengers had spoken to me seventeen years before.

Perhaps my lessons on energy had begun much earlier through the often-subconscious level of dreams. Learning the life review served to release the final Earth energies makes sense now but not when the dream had occurred. I realized that truth may lie buried beneath the surface of awareness, but time has a way of uncovering it. Would truth always come to light? I returned my attention to the December 2013 message:

In reference to the [2002] dream, the life review is a part of the events that occur when a human loses its Life Force Energy, and the physical body is no longer required. When the physical body dies, the energy body is released; it is freed. For there to be complete freedom, old energy particles are sloughed off and released to reach the divine spark or soul or spirit within. It is the releasing of the energy packets, molecules, or clouds that are part of the steps necessary for a complete transition to free the spirit.

All thoughts and memories are energy. When these energies are released, ideas and memories are also released, thus causing the human to review their life. It is done rapidly since there is no longer a dense physical body to hold the energy packets together. This is why humans say that their life flashes in front of their eyes. There is a literal flash on a subatomic level.

The recently released energy body still carries the thoughts and life experiences through memories from the Earth plane. Thoughts are contained as energy packets. As these packets detach from the newly released energy body, the energies, through thoughts and memories, are released and become the life review.

Although I had known these memory spheres were the basis of the life review, I had not known why. My training as a psychologist made it easy to understand how reviewing memories offered insight and learning opportunities from our actions. From the perspective of energy, I also realized the benefit of releasing suppressed frequencies, but this December 2013 message suggested another essential reason for the life review: physics.

The life review releases the dense Earth plane energies—a requirement for the person's spirit to return to its source. The memory orbs must disengage from the physical body for the complete transition to occur.

My awareness wove through the threads of time from the dream in 2002 to the messages in 2013, 2014, and 2019. I began to understand how the intertwined pieces had given me insight into fundamental questions about life and death. Had this information arrived with the 2002 dream, I would not have understood its divine wisdom and truth.

Since my spontaneous opening to spirit in August 2013, I've felt as if angelic forces have silently orchestrated my life, pulling threads from the past to weave a multidimensional tapestry that is often beyond my comprehension. The journey has sometimes been slow, arduous, and often disjointed, but I've come to realize information flowed in the manner in which it was designed, including when I was ready to accept it.

As I continue my path of discovery, I realize how much I have changed. Behind is everything I knew or thought I knew, yet a more significant part of me has moved forward. Little jewels of wisdom and insight artfully hide among the dreams, thoughts, and messages we receive every day, but until we are ready to see them, they drop by the wayside. We don't lose these gems of wisdom; they are always there, waiting for us to perceive them. Learning to see through the eyes of the heart opens us to the divine guidance surrounding us.

As we prepare to traverse the unknown ways of 2020, let us remember to follow the wisdom of our hearts, knowing our angels are here to help us.

CHAPTER 5: NEVER ALONE

S ome events are so deeply embedded in your mind that no matter how much time passes, the details don't fade. While many memories are a jumbled collection of fragmented moments, these stories are like whispers that burst through consciousness when you least expect it, catapulting you back in time with dramatic precision. My date to remember was September 2, 1987.

It was a date of profound loss, but I later discovered truth may lie beneath the surface, buried and forgotten until time uncovers it. Eventually, I found the proverbial silver lining, and a glimmer of hope surfaced, piercing the clouds of darkness. That flicker grew until light shone through with blinding force, and my despair transformed to comfort and strength when I learned we are never alone. Never.

September 2, 1987. Less than four months after my husband's thirty-fifth birthday, I was keeping vigil over him at Lourdes Hospital in Paducah, Kentucky. The cancer had spread, and Daryl would soon transition from this life.

I took a short break to get a cup of coffee from the Intensive Care's spacious waiting room, a place that had served as my source of refuge for the past five days. I noticed two new visitors who sat side by side, facing the picture window overlooking the city.

Fall was a few weeks away, but already the tree-covered banks of the Ohio River that separated Kentucky from Illinois were dressed in autumn colors. Beyond the river, the hills unfolded in a magnificent display of reds, yellows, and golds.

I'm not sure why I paid attention to these gray-haired men, but I did. They seemed out of place as they peacefully gazed through the large window. They didn't have the vacuous glassy-eyed or disheveled appearance of the rest of us.

I glanced in their direction when one of the men stated he had seen an angel on a busy street corner in Cincinnati, Ohio. He lifted his arm as he described the angel's flight into the sky. There was a brief pause. He turned to his friend, chuckled, and said, "The angel had wings on his feet."

An angel with winged feet? I rolled my eyes at the comment and smiled in response to this nonsense. I picked up my still-steaming cup of coffee and walked the long corridor back to Daryl's room.

I opened the door and stood for a few moments to gaze at my husband's lifeless body. Tears flooded my eyes; I knew his time to pass was approaching. He was the love of my life. I didn't want to lose him, but I couldn't bear to witness his pain as he struggled with each breath. I sighed deeply, walked to his bed, and placed my hand on top of his.

My thoughts were interrupted when the hospital's chaplain entered. Through my sobs, I asked him to pray for Daryl's release from suffering. Father Dillard held my free hand and placed his other hand on my husband. As he began to pray, a wave of peace washed over me as his message echoed throughout the stillness of the room. These words felt holy and sacred. I breathed deeply and sank into the serenity that surrounded his hallowed prayer.

My eyes flew open when the chaplain summoned the angels with winged feet to carry Daryl home. Hearing about these angelic beings twice within one hour stunned me, yet on a level deep within my soul, I knew this was true. A short time later, surrounded by family, the angels fulfilled the chaplain's request to escort my beloved into the afterlife.

The gray-haired men and the chaplain speaking of angels with winged feet felt mystical, and it defied any explanation I had. It was years before I told anyone about these events. In my heart, I knew there was sacred knowledge embedded within these memories, yet its hidden secret was something I couldn't begin to understand, so I remained quiet, waiting for meaning to surface.

Years passed, and for reasons I can no longer recall, I shared the incident with my sister Eleanore. She immediately identified the men in the hospital's waiting room as the angels who ushered Daryl into the afterlife. They had manifested as two gray-haired men who were biding their time until he was ready to transition.

Eleanore repeated the Bible verse (King James Version) in Hebrews 13:2: "Be not forgetful to entertain strangers: for thereby some have entertained angels unaware." Almost twenty-seven years later, in a message on May 13, 2014, the angels verified what my sister had told me. Those gray-haired gentlemen were angels.

When I had first seen them in the waiting room, I had sensed something different about them. The men seemed out of place. I had thought their conversation about angels with winged feet was absurd until the hospital chaplain summoned those same angels minutes later.

Was there a lesson here? I realized more than ever that answers are already present, merely awaiting to be unveiled. Knowledge comes in mysterious ways and often not through words that require our five senses to interpret. You cannot always talk about it, but you can see and feel it. You have to go above the material world to find some truths.

My ever-expanding belief system opens the door for higher truths. As I gradually discover more of my inner being, I enter a field of peace and contentment as I learn to experience life through a broader perspective. Words are not necessary, for it is the life experiences that color in more detail of truth.

Knowing angels had manifested in human form was invaluable, and it made my relationship with them more personal. But learning that love transcends our Earthly existence had a more significant impact on me. When we drop our physical forms to transition to the afterlife, our true essence continues; we do not die.

What happens when we transition? Do we become angels or guides? Do we watch over our loved ones who remain behind, or do we move on to other places or dimensions? These questions played in the back of my mind early one morning.

I had taken a short beach walk before breakfast. I was showered and dressed, getting ready to step into my role as Nana. Shortly after noon, I'd need to leave the house to pick up Shalane from her prekindergarten class. I loved balancing my life as a retired psychologist with my duties as a grandmother.

As what frequently happens with the messengers, my thoughts seemed to offer a silent invitation for a reply from other-worldly sources. I had enough time to sit at the computer, open my messages document, and type the following:

March 15, 2019

Yes, and yes, we say. Sometimes, and sometimes not, we say. It is difficult to describe what happens when there is a transition to our dimension because the full description is beyond what humans are capable of understanding.

It is not that humans lack the intellect; they lack the awareness or re-membrance of living in the nonphysical dimension of pure energy. Entering Earth plane existence creates a veil of forgetfulness, so they do not have the understanding or even the vocabulary to describe in a manner in which there is full comprehension.

The messengers had previously mentioned the veil of forgetfulness. It is an interdimensional space between Earth and the nonphysical realms. The angels had said the veil created the perception of separation, but in reality, there is only unity. The message continued:

When humans drop their physical forms, they revert to their formless nature, similar to what or who they were before they incarnated. They are not the same as before because Earth plane experience adds layers to their previous state, building upon the previously established foundation.

As humans experience life in the Earth plane, there is also a discarding of parts that are outdated and no longer useful. Much like human technology, the changes are similar to updating a computer's operating system.

I liked this concept of building life lessons and how these experiences help to upgrade our spiritual operating system. It made sense. The message continued:

When humans initially enter our realm, they meet with other souls who welcome them to their new homes. The first to arrive are often family members or close friends who had preceded them in this transition. They are part of what we call the transition team.

This is not the first contact with the transition teams. Before the human's final transition, the team will visit—sometimes in dreams, sometimes during waking states. On some occasions, we interact with the others surrounding those preparing to transition.

79

Many humans believe that these are hallucinations, but that is not the case. When the human body is in transition, their physical senses change. No longer limited, they begin to step into the glorified body of the next dimension. They begin to sense differently. The physical eyes are no longer the only organs that can see. The physical ears are no longer the only organs that can hear.

Transition teams seemed logical to me and even why or how they could occur. I had read about deathbed visions where the soon-to-be departed saw and sometimes communicated with others who had passed. Often these nonphysical visitors helped escort their loved ones into the afterlife.

As the physical form slips into the nonphysical, consciousness expands. The spiritual senses open, and we finally see, hear, and feel more intensely than we do with our limited human faculties.

Approaching this final stage in our lives creates warp-speed evolution that takes us to the threshold of beyond, opening extraordinary spaces past the outer edges of human consciousness. As thrilling as this sounds, having a transition team to help guide us through these passages comforted me.

The idea of transition teams is logical, but I was curious about their interactions with the bystanders of those preparing to transition. I searched online for more information.

Although not as common as near-death experiences, shared-death experiences include other participants in the transition process.[8] According to SharedCrossing.com, it's not just loved ones who are involved, but caregivers and sometimes bystanders. Those events range from an out-of-body experience as the other person dies, co-experiencing the life review of the one transitioning, seeing beings of light or a heavenly place, or encountering other-

---

8 www.sharedcrossing.com/shared-death-experience.html

worldly sensory input like geometric designs, mist, or music. The angels continued:

> *Members of the transition team include us, the angels. We are the overseers of the process. Some guides help lay the foundation of the path for the human to follow. Because the human in the transition state is between dimensions, it is easier for them to connect with loved ones who had previously departed. There are also many lightworkers on the Earth plane who assist in this process as well.*
>
> *There are many types of energies in our dimension, not just the souls of departed humans. Our dimension contains the blueprint for all Earth plane energies. All living entities on the Earth plane stem from this masterplan. Trees, mountains, oceans, plains, deserts, mammals, fish, fowl, and minerals all have their foundations within our dimension. The master plan exists in our realm.*

I thought of famous works of art. As the name suggests, inspirational masterpieces have supernatural or divine origins. Is the blueprint in the celestial realm while the manifestation on Earth is a primitive model of the original? The message continued:

> *Our dimension is your home. Many humans who have had what are called near-death experiences report a sense of homecoming. We say to you that it is because, even if for a brief time, they have reconnected with other aspects of themselves that they may not have been aware of when occupying the physical body. Their existence on the Earth plane is but a shadow of a thought of their full selves. The original is in our dimension.*
>
> *Transition to our realm is a grand homecoming, indeed, as the human steps into the fullness of their true self. The totality*

of their divine nature cannot exist in the Earth plane. The energy is too intense for the human body to tolerate. However, this is changing. As Earth continues transitioning to higher dimensions, humans can accept more energy into their physical bodies.

The veil is lifting. It is part of the evolution of your species.

There was a lot of material to unpack from the message. The veil of forgetfulness serves multiple purposes. It allows us to enter this marvelous planet with a blank slate. We disconnect from our all-knowing, higher selves, and are left to our own devices (or so we think) to learn lessons. As we evolve, we begin to understand the more magnificent, often subtler aspects of life.

The veil of forgetfulness serves another, less philosophical purpose, one steeped in the realm of physicality: Our human forms cannot tolerate the expansive frequencies of our higher selves. The veil serves as a filtering mechanism, allowing only those energies we can endure.

The angel spoke of Earth's transition to higher dimensions. Reviewing this message through the May 2020 mid-pandemic lens, I now understand the angels had been speaking of current times. We are at the precipice of Mother Earth's evolutionary transition to higher dimensions, traveling on her coattails. As she evolves, we evolve.

This shift for humanity and our blue-green planet takes us one step closer to our greater selves. As the interdimensional veil thins, our physical bodies will change, and we'll be able to accept higher frequencies. Our lives can become richer.

As we evolve with Mother Earth, we will see the greater picture. Will we accept Gaia's call for unity? Will we see her as a living entity? Will we take responsibility for our actions? Will we understand humanity is only one aspect of our beautiful planet? The choices are ours to make.

I finished recording the message in my online journal and glanced at my watch. It was time to shut down the computer and pick up Shalane. I gathered my purse and headed to the car. During the twelve-minute ride to her prekindergarten class, thoughts about the message flooded my mind. Why me? I often wondered why I had been chosen to receive these cosmic communications. I don't describe myself as unique or gifted; I'm an ordinary person who has tapped into the subtle realms of spirit. The thinning of the veil, as part of humanity's evolution, seemed to suggest at least a partial answer to my often-asked question.

The weakening of dimensional barriers offered me opportunities to receive valuable information about life, the transition process, and life after death. There is so much more to this world than what our physical senses can measure. We are expansive, divine beings, only to have forgotten our origins as we passed through the veil of forgetfulness to become part of the human race.

The veil's thinning uncovers universal truths. The lessons we learn on Earth, our life experiences, add to the total sum of who we are. These events offer an upgrade to our basic spiritual operating systems. Hopefully, we exit this lifetime with fresh material, raising our energy vibrations.

As we grow, and as the dimensional space between here and hereafter fades, we begin to see life as it is. We know the unity. We understand the guidance of angels and others. We feel the comfort from our other-worldly transition teams who guide us through our births and who escort us back into the nonphysical, back to our true homes.

I pulled into the parking lot of Shalane's school and exited the car. When I heard the laughter of children, I realized the class was on the playground. As I entered the side gate, the look on Shalane's face told me she was having too much fun to stop. After more than a little bit of coaxing and a promise to help her make a special present for Lorelai when she got off the school bus, we headed to the car.

Over a week later, I woke with angels on my mind. Although not fully alert, I found myself sinking in thoughts of these celestial beings and their messages. I popped out of bed and went straight to the computer to capture my ideas.

The first thought I had was that we are never alone. Never. Angels guide us throughout our lives. I feel honored and blessed to be able to glimpse at the fuller picture of who we are, but I was curious. Who are the angels?

I've had many conversations with nonphysical entities since 2013, and most messengers were unidentified. Some gave a name or location, but the majority remained anonymous. Because the wisdom of their words took precedence over their identities, I had little desire to learn who they were until the angels told me about their names.

I searched my online document to find the date. It was May 2015 when I learned angel names are vibratory signatures. As humans, we respond to our names because of conditioning. When we react to our names as infants, we receive hugs, smiles, and lots of attention. It's the classic behavioral training of stimulus and response.

It's different with angels; there is no need for prior conditioning. Angelic names are part of their energy field and these frequencies entrain to voice signals. It's a stronger bond than classical conditioning because the automatic connection is as natural as the pull of magnets. No more searching the crowd for the source of the call; the link is immediate.

As the information flowed into my awareness, I realized how much I had learned about the angelic realm. Although I may not have always reached out to discover their names, the energy was unmistakable, often manifesting in my mind's eye as intricate ribbons of pastel pinks and greens that waft through the air like slow-motion chiffon scarves.

The most reliable indicators of angels, however, are my physical and emotional reactions. I feel the distinct and often awe-inspiring energies of love, gratitude, compassion, and strength. As angels enter my awareness, my senses are on high alert. My breath quickens, and my heart pounds, often followed by a flood of tears.

I know angels often surround me, yet if I always felt their presence, it would disrupt my day-to-day activities. How do they guide me yet filter their almost-overwhelming energies? As I pondered this question, the answer arrived. They used an intermediary.

While still seated at the computer, I opened my messages journal to record the following clarification:

March 26, 2019

Each human has a higher self. The higher self operates as a direct link between the Earth plane existence and our dimension. The higher self is more directly connected to the human than we are, thus making it easier for the human to communicate and benefit from higher-dimensional energies.

We, the angels, connect to a human by way of the higher self. We are not the only higher-dimensional energies to do so, but this is our primary access. The higher self operates as an interdimensional filter. It reduces our frequencies that might prove to be disruptive to the human's daily experiences, their lessons in life. Because of this filtering mechanism, humans can proceed without interruption.

We have a direct link to the higher self of each living being. Our realm oversees all living things—everything with a life force, not just mammals. The higher self is individualized to a specific organism; it is particular to each energy system. Humans often interpret guidance as "self-talk," not their consciousness speaking. But that is not so.

It is the individual connection, the personal connection, that makes the relationship possible. When our help is requested, we respond directly, and our response results in a vibrational overflow from the higher self. Because of the filtering mechanism, our energy engulfs the human energy field. This results in an interruption of daily activities and can interfere with the lessons the human may experience.

The higher self is that constant connection to us, for it allows the activities of daily living without overwhelming energy input.

This communique reinforced that we are never alone. The constant connection to the angels via the higher self serves to counterbalance energies from the angel realm. But the message sparked something within—the realization of how these new messages continued to shape my beliefs. I began to color outside the lines of my old life as, message by message, I offered up old views to a clearer light and discarded many tenets of my past.

I looked at the clock. I'd spent almost two hours at the computer, and I hadn't showered or even had coffee. I saved my documents, closed the computer, then prepared for the rest of my day.

While in the shower, I felt the silent calling from a messenger. Over the years, I've grown accustomed to these nudges. When I least expected it, an errant thought would cross my mind, often requiring me to search previous messages.

I might have ignored these thoughts in the past, but I had come to recognize them as a prompt from a messenger. I knew to pay attention. I dried off, dressed, and headed to the kitchen. After making a cup of pour-over coffee, I'd be ready for the search.

Following the unspoken urge from minutes before, I opened

my messages journal and typed "higher self" in the search bar. Within seconds, the following older entry filled my computer's screen:

June 20, 2014

This one has questions about what is referred to as a higher self. What does it mean to channel information from your higher source or higher self? Each human has their own higher source depending upon the specific energy makeup of that source. This one has been given the analogy of a cluster of grapes.

Each grape cluster represents a lifetime, and the newest growth signifies the current life. Yet it is not in isolation, for this topmost cluster represents new expansion from the trunk and roots; it is the culmination of all lives as aspects flow from one lifetime to another. The individual grapes on clusters represent experiences associated with that specific life.

I have connected with numerous nonphysical entities since 2013, and I knew each possessed a unique vibration. This message suggested we could use our intentions to tap into specific frequencies. Like selecting a grape from a cluster, we can choose which energy packet to explore. This process allows us to delve into details of previous lifetimes.

When I had received the message in 2014, I'd been surprised by the references to past lives. Now I view reincarnation through the lens of energy, making it easier to comprehend and accept that our true essence lives through numerous lifetimes. I returned to the 2014 message:

We have been a part of this one's existence in the past. This is why there is a connection to her. There is an energy connection and, thus, an attraction.

The message answers a question in the back of my mind that I had not yet articulated. I understand how the soul continues through various incarnations, but what about our higher selves? Does that connection between us and the angelic realm also remain consistent between lifetimes?

The message suggests that it does. Our lives, including past lives, are guided by our higher selves. The higher self is our primary guidance system, and it strengthens with each incarnation. It is our link to the angels, regardless of the lifetime.

Understanding how the higher self will guide us through the various iterations of the soul's journey added clarity to the messenger's grape analogy. The branches connecting the clusters to the arm of the vine represent the higher self. Lessons learned from past lives upload to the trunk and become fodder for future lives. Once in the trunk of the vine, these experiences result in an evolutionary spurt in our operating systems.

Just as pruning foliage from a grapevine promotes growth, as we discard beliefs that no longer serve us, we become more vibrant. What remains are the essential elements needed for transformation. Our operating systems improve and evolve with each incarnation's pruning as we upload these vital components of those lives.

I couldn't help but marvel at this—not the concept but my level of comfort with it. Over the years, my nonordinary conversations and visions had pushed against the boundaries of my beliefs. I recalled my fear and confusion when the first messenger arrived in August 2013, yet day by day, message by message, my ideology changed. And just when I thought my belief system had stretched to its limit, new information broke through my linear thinking. Yet this was an easy process. My adventures into the unknown were composed of small, incremental steps that gently led me down this path of mystery and intrigue. The 2014 message continued:

In energy terms, think of a darkened space. Then, there is a very slight and subtle thread of energy or awareness. Some humans may see this as a tiny, silver thread or filament of energy, or perhaps they may sense the presence by feeling it. Others may feel a slight tingling in the atmosphere, as if a section is vibrating at a different rate. This subtle thread of energy leads back to its source. It attracts the awareness of its kind. A human who had once been a part of this specific source will be drawn to it, for it is part of the source from whence the human came.

The vision that had accompanied the initial message began to replay in my mind's eye. I was in the pitch-black silent void of a cave as swirls of hypnagogic images of different shades of black danced around me. A glimmer of light caught my attention. It looked like a small luminous silk thread, but it was more than that. I knew it was alive; it had life-force energy within.

If I focused on this wiggling fiber, it disappeared, only to reappear when I looked away. It seemed to be aware of my movements and thoughts. That piqued my interest, so I experimented. I stopped chasing it, and instead, I sent forth a request to connect. The thread of light responded, moving closer like a timid animal that recognizes friendship. The more positive energy I sent, the closer it came. The message continued:

To tap into your higher source, humans must sit in silence and wait for the awareness to come—wait for that disturbance in the energy field to approach their area of consciousness and show itself.

When one sits in silence, humans often report a deep, velvety void. After sitting in the void and becoming comfortable with it, the nonphysical senses begin to accommodate to the darkness and stillness. At this point, there is a beginning of recognition of energy strands, which are often perceived in contrast to darkness.

Some humans can see these strands. Other humans feel them. Others simply know these strands are there. When humans sit in the silence and darkness, they exist in nonordinary reality. Their nonphysical senses drive their awareness and, thus, they perceive differences in energy patterns. Their own source energy is attracted to them if they remain still and open.

Had this occurred with me in the vision? While sitting in silence, I had used my nonphysical senses to attract these strands, allowing them to connect with my source energy.

I didn't know what all of this meant. What was the lesson? Was this just an exercise in understanding how nonphysical senses affect energy filaments? By learning how to communicate with these atypical energy systems, did this serve as practice for other connections? I didn't know, but I was willing to learn more. The message continued:

Using the nonphysical senses, each human's awareness is individualized. What is essential to know is that the perception, regardless of which sense they use to recognize the strand, is true for them. It is their specific source that is making the connection, coming full circle to connect with that which was lost. If they trust and follow the link, it will become stronger, making future contacts easier, leading them back to the source of the active thread.

The review of this 2014 message brought new information to light. I realized how much I had changed. The ancient wisdom of the messengers had opened interdimensional doorways, and I found myself far beyond my beginning point. I felt astonished as

I realized I consider things like past lives as fact instead of theory. Yes, I had undoubtedly stretched my belief system beyond its previous state. The messengers had transformed me, and these changes had enriched my life beyond measure.

These changes in perception allow me to paint outside the lines of my once-linear thinking. With a new perspective, I see things differently. I realize there are particular moments that define each one of us. We may not recognize it at the time, but we do later. Every action creates cascades of reactions that intertwine in a web of events called life, but truth always surfaces.

Because we experience life through the lens of personal history, our inability to conceive of new things holds us back. However, evidence will weave itself across the fabric of life to offer different views. You can put your finger on it, that definable, indelible moment when everything changes.

Although I had not recognized it in real-time, that unforgettable moment was September 2, 1987, the date my husband died. It was a day of profound loss and sorrow, but later I discovered its broader context: peace that surpasses understanding. This was the date of my encounter with two angels disguised as grayed-haired men; the moment I learned we are not alone.

As the years pass, the past, present, and future dissolve within one another, exposing the truth that lies dormant beneath the sands of time. Neither time nor truth are as linear as I once had thought. I now know transition teams of angels surround us from before birth. Throughout our daily lives, we connect to this divine guidance through our higher selves.

Many of us cling to the belief that our final transition will be a solo journey, but a higher consciousness says otherwise. It had taken years for me to discover I had first-hand knowledge. After all, I had seen the angels with my own eyes.

When it's time to return to the nonphysical realms that had once been home, we will not be alone. We will slip into the next dimension together with our angels, returning hand in hand, to the place we once called home. Together. Never alone.

CHAPTER 6: THE SERAPH

T he darkness of midnight blew through the open window. Where was I? I glanced at my surroundings. The house was Victorian, but what was I doing here? I glanced at my clothes: a collared, long-sleeved off-white cotton nightgown that buttoned down the front. It was straight from the mid-1800s.

I floated two or three feet off the ground, the tips of my toes visible beneath the floor-length nightdress. While dangling in midair, my perspective changed, and I found myself observing from a position near the ceiling.

Several angels glided around me, blowing gently on my suspended body. Looking from one end of the room to the other, the observer-me saw a tube of medicine on the candlelit bedside table. "Seraphim" was written on the label, and I immediately knew this was a healing balm created by seraphim angels.

I soon discovered this dream was a prelude of what was to come: face-to-face visits with these angelic beings. I began to understand that dreams aren't meaningless visualizations; they can represent doorways into other dimensions. Because our doubts and egos are tucked away from our awareness during sleep, we allow these events to unfold naturally. With our logical and judgmental minds aside, we allow guidance from spirit to enter.

This contact with the seraphim had begun in May 2015. I'd registered for a series of angel classes at Goddess I Am hosted by Sandra McGill. When the first session ended, I drove the short distance home, and as I prepared for bed, I thought about the next day's work schedule.

As a psychologist in the public-school system, my plate was already full before the mid-May last-minute requests for psychological evaluations. I'm very organized, and I knew I'd finish everything, but it would take some fancy maneuvering to do so.

I set the alarm for 4:40 a.m. and dropped into bed, but I tossed and turned for almost an hour before successfully fending off thoughts of tomorrow's hectic schedule. After one more resolute glance at the clock, I finally drifted to sleep, but not before images from the angel class invaded my mind. Those last waking thoughts must have opened the doors for my angelic visitors; I woke before the alarm, dreaming of me in the Victorian bedroom with the seraphim.

I jumped from bed and ran to the computer to document the details while they were on my mind. After showering and a quick bowl of Cheerios, I grabbed my go-cup of coffee and walked out the door at 6:10. I was ready to meet the day of back-to-back meetings.

It was busy, another one of those no-lunch Tuesdays. Within the brief pauses between appointments, I thought about the dream. It was so real. The following day, the messengers spoke about their previous night's visit:

May 13, 2015

This one experienced the breath of angels in her dream. Angels are watching over you at all times. Most humans do not recognize this fact, for the presence of angels is like a whisper or a shadow of a thought. It is like a gentle breeze that carries the fragrance of a blossom into awareness. The presence is always there, but the recognition requires stillness and silence—a "tuning in."

The fragrance from the breeze stems from the heart of Mother Earth, just as this one experienced the gentle breath of angels. To recognize angelic guidance, an energy match is required—an overlap of vibrational frequencies. This is why connections to angels most often occur during times of stillness and silence such as prayer, meditation, or dream states.

We came to this one in her dream in acknowledgment of her reconnection with us [during the angel class]. *We are ever-present, watching over our beloved humans. As Mother Earth continues her ascension into higher realms, we see, with excitement, humans making connections with us. We rejoice and are filled with glee when we see these conscious connections.*

We are here with you; we are here for you. Members of our realm have been with you since before you entered the world of human physicality. We will continue with you, guiding and protecting you throughout your human life. We will be with you when you drop your physical body and join us in spirit. At that time, there will be rejoicing for this homecoming, for those parts of you that have forgotten, you will remember. There will be full recognition as you re-member with us.

Not remembering us is not a function of the human brain, but instead, it is a function of the density of your vibratory existence in the Earth plane. When the physical body drops its presence in the Earth plane, your lighter, more vibrant, spirit or soul will soar.

The lighter, more delicate vibrations of the newly released human spirit seek its vibrational match. The radiating energy of the angelic realm acts both as a beacon and a magnet, calling and guiding those recently released souls to return home. That is all for now.

The message validated the significance of the dream, and I was eager to share it with my classmates, but how could I? I had not divulged my ability to receive messages from the nonphysical. I felt the sting of confliction, so I compromised and decided to email Sandra the details of my dream and the corresponding words from the messengers.

Although they seemed significant, I doubted myself. Maybe the dream wasn't that special, and my experience was commonplace. Perhaps the others in the class had similar encounters. The next session would be in five days; I'd let Sandra decide whether or not to share it with the group. Taking a deep breath, not knowing whether I was ready to reveal my well-kept secret, I hit the send button.

Half a week later, I walked in the door at Goddess I Am for the second class, and my ears perked when I heard Sandra mention seraphim to another student. My heart pounded when I thought she was talking about my email, but I was wrong. I gleaned from the conversation that Sandra was referring to another series of classes called Seraphim Blueprint. I smiled as I realized this was yet another message involving seraphim angels.

Several weeks after the final class ended, I couldn't stop thinking about the seraphim. Through dreams, messages, and overheard conversations, they had stepped from the shadows and into my awareness. Perhaps it was time to discover why I had been led to learn about these angels.

I began with an online search. Seraphim, according to Seraphim Blueprint founder Ruth Rendely, are a "group of high angels" who created a cosmology for the "well-being and evolution" of humanity.[9] This cosmology was created thirteen thousand years ago and resurfaced in 1994 when one of the original angels contacted Rendely.

The Seraphim Blueprint is available on four continents for face-to-face meetings, or they can be accessed via the Internet. Throughout the six classes, eleven distinct energies are introduced through initiations that work on the physical, emotional, mental, and spiritual levels of the participants.

Imagine my surprise to find an active group of teachers here in Naples, Florida. I couldn't help but smile at yet another seraphim synchronicity. I knew this was the way of guidance. One step leads to another, and before you know it, a new path unfolds. It seemed the universe had paved the way, and it was my destiny to learn more about these divine beings.

Time seemed to slip by, and as I marked off the July days from my calendar, I realized the summer break from school would soon end. It was time to get serious about the seraphim who had mysteriously made their presence known in my life. I contacted one of the trainers who agreed to hold a class in my two-bedroom apartment.

Because of the limited space, this was a small class with just my close friends, Scott and Maria, who had agreed to join me on this adventure. As I tidied my living room in preparation for the first session, I wondered how these initiations would work. Were they similar to the downloads I sometimes receive from the messengers where the entire information arrives at once?

I'd been gathering verifiable information from nonphysical realms for almost two years at this point, yet a healthy dose of skepticism remained. How could someone become a conduit for angels? Would these initiations accomplish what founder Ruth Rendely claims? How would I know if the activations were

---

9 https://www.seraphimblueprint.org/Home/

authentic? I soon found out.

Gigi Peterson, the instructor for the first few classes, arrived early, followed shortly by Scott and Maria. While Gigi prepared for this day-long program, Maria and I staked our claims to use the two couches. Scott graciously accepted blankets and a pillow for the floor.

It was time to begin. I was snuggled in the couch with a light blanket and my journal and pencil at my side. Gigi had us relax and close our eyes as she brought forth the first initiation. Within seconds, I felt familiar energy vibrations, the same frequencies I'd become accustomed to when connecting to nonphysical sources.

The first surge entered my feet, moved up my legs and into my arms. I picked up the pencil and sketched a stick figure of myself. I drew wiggling arrows at my feet to signify where the pulsing vibrations had begun.

In my mind's eye, I saw a soft purple mist rise from the palms of my hands. Tiny particles from the outer layer of my energy body combined with this amethyst-colored fog, molding it into a purple ray. An understanding entered my awareness, and I knew this beam linked me with the seraphim energies guided by Gigi. With the connection established, the first message arrived:

July 25, 2015

We have always been connected, but you have not always allowed yourself to experience and acknowledge this divine connection. Much like an umbilical cord, the function of the purple ray is to strengthen and nurture as a mother nourishes her soon-to-be offspring. You are a divine spark, a part of the wholeness of us. We give you strength, love, and aliveness. It is with pleasure and deep abiding love and gratitude that we acknowledge the connectivity that you have now experienced.

The familiar sensations of energy, the visions, and the message validated for me the authenticity of the seraphim. What had been synchronistic associations in the first angel class had morphed into a genuine connection. I intuitively knew the purple mist, at least for me, signified the seraphim's presence.

Energy from angels is unique and easily recognizable. Although I typically saw pinks and greens when they were present, this was not the case with the seraphim. Beginning with this first initiation and throughout the entire six classes, the purple mist became the conduit for accessing them. It was always there. It became their calling card, and it remains so today.

The second exercise was as profound as the first. Energy streamed up and down my spinal cord, so I detailed that in my journal by using heavy marks in the center of my penciled body. As these new frequencies coursed through me, I understood it was building the foundation, enabling me to accept more seraphim energies.

The third initiation brought a gentle wave of frequencies to the center of my back that split into two currents near my shoulder blades. These twin torrents arched approximately three feet from my back before returning to an area just above my hips. As I added these details to my drawing, a message came:

Each waveform becomes a passage of ever-looping, ever-flowing energy from the divine. As this loop of divine power continues to flow, its pathway becomes strengthened. The path from self to source is enhanced, thus allowing these divine frequencies to permeate your body and beyond. It is a connection that, once started, never ends. Yes, for allowing is the energy of receiving. Those frequencies match and allow for the oneness, which is beginning to flow.

Not only did these loops strengthen with each shoulder-

99

blades-to-hips orbit, they produced significant heat. I felt as if I were in a sauna. I kicked off my blanket, but it didn't seem to help. When I thought I couldn't tolerate any more heat, the energy burst through the top of my head as if forced through an escape hatch, creating a giant ring of steam above me.

I picked up my pencil and drew wavy arrows near my head to signify the path of the energy movement. As I sketched the energy ring above me, another message arrived:

The energy is strong and powerful. As it meets with the sacred ground of Mother Earth, it grows in strength. Combining our radiance with that of Mother Earth forms a protective seal which stabilizes this energy of light within your body. The bottoms of your feet serve as the foundation, creating a magnetic pull for the energy to be attracted to you. The angel-Earth union creates a magnetic effect that maintains the balance of these new energies of light to remain within you.

The rise in my body temperature confirmed the strength of the energy. As I thought about the message's connection to Mother Earth, I realized the first activation had begun with intense vibrations at my feet. This must have been the foundational connection to Mother Earth the messenger referenced.

Gigi announced it was time for a bio break. I sat up and stretched as I looked at my notes and thought about the initiations. Each wave of energy was different, yet there was a noticeable progression from purple mist on my hands to energy spirals on my back to a smoldering smoke ring above my head. Not knowing the purpose of these frequencies didn't stop my eagerness to continue.

I looked at my artistic attempt to depict each activation, and I passed the sketch around the room. As Gigi, Scott, and Maria viewed my primitive art, Scott made an announcement that surprised me. He stated I had drawn an angel.

As we took turns considering the picture, we knew Scott's interpretation was correct. It was apparent, yet I had been completely oblivious. My first design was a line-drawn body of me, and exercise by exercise, I had depicted incoming energy by a progressive series of arrows, circles, and wavy markings. The loops from my shoulder blades to my hips resembled wings, and the above-the-head ring of mist from the escape valve looked like a halo.

I had superimposed an angel over a line-drawn body of me. By sketching what occurred during the downloads, by my own hands, I had become an angel, yet I had remained completely unaware.

I looked closer at the picture. As I tried to comprehend how I failed to see this obvious connection, another revelation surprised me. I had drawn three sets of wavy lines to represent the energy clusters at my feet, back, and head, and each set looked like wings. I didn't have wings only on my back, they were also at my head and my feet. I was an angel with three sets of wings.

Several months later, I researched seraphim angels and was astounded to discover they have three sets of wings. Isaiah 6:2 of the King James Version of the Bible describes the seraphim with wings on their backs, feet, and heads—precisely where I had sketched them. I could only chuckle at this after-the-fact research that confirmed my experience.

The break ended, and Maria, Scott, and I were eager to receive the remaining initiations. I intuitively knew the first few exercises had prepared me for what was to come. These activations had installed the seraphim frequencies in my energy field, and the following activities would build on that foundation.

The next few downloads were intense and vivid. I saw a series of small balls that floated within my body. These had purposefully detached from the vibrational waves from the previous exercises. I heard they were "vibrational satellites," and they carried the frequencies of the earlier initiations' attunements.

I did not understand what that meant until I experienced it. Within seconds, the satellites zipped through my energy body, cleansing it. These angelic orbs permeated me on a cellular level. I sank deep into a beautiful blanket of energy, feeling calm, comforted, and protected.

I rested within this divine space while these satellites realigned my energy field. Tingles, buzzing, stomach grumbles, and other vibrations coursed through my body, making way for the sacred and healing energies of the seraphim.

The vibrations stopped as quickly as they had begun, followed by what felt like a slow-moving glacier of energy. It slid from the top of my head to the bottoms of my feet, covering my entire body. I had an intuitive knowing this action sealed the installed seraphim energies within me. What had begun with a purple ray was complete.

Gigi called for another break before the final transmission. It was nearing dinner time, and I could not believe how quickly the day had passed. I'd received so much information from this first session. I couldn't believe there would be five more classes in the Seraphim Blueprint program.

After a quick trip to the restroom, a handful of snacks, and several gulps of water, I was ready for the final initiation. As the activation began, energy ballooned from the center of my chest to twelve or fourteen inches beyond my physical body. A glorious wave washed over me as vibrations of grace, sweetness, and love circulated. I felt it in every fiber of my being. It was as if I were inside a chrysalis, awaiting transformation.

The energies strengthened. I felt intense itching in the middle of my forehead; at the same time, a swirling vortex surrounded my heart. I took a deep breath as profound restorative energy permeated me.

I looked at my right hand and was surprised to see a tattoo

of a ring on my finger. As the observer-me pulled back, the me in the vision sat lotus style in midair in a vacuum of rainbow-colored lights. The spectrum of energy morphed into multiple shades of purple. I knew I was in a sacred and divine space, but where? The seraphim spoke:

> *It is with open arms that we welcome you into this space, which is most holy and sacred. It is with an open heart that we extend our healing energies to you. Go forth, shine, be that beacon.*
>
> *Use your energy gifts for healing, not only for humankind, but for plants, minerals, animals, and your most precious Earth.*

This energy exchange was intense and sweat streamed down my face. I tossed my blanket to the side while scribbling my notes from this rapid download of information. Things beyond my understanding poured in. I had glimpses of my soul's purpose and being in harmony with the universe. I heard the words "Buddha facilitation with the divine." I had no idea what that phrase meant but only that things beyond my comprehension were becoming part of my energy field. Perhaps these seeds of knowledge would manifest when and if I became ready to comprehend them.

Thousands of points of light entered my hands and feet, drifted to my trunk, and crossed my body. My physical form seemed to unravel as I entered a state of at-one-ment with all that is. I felt my real essence spread, gliding across the universe.

I was no longer separate. I was everything. My thoughts and actions manifested as ripples across the cosmos in a symbiotic dance that was the basis for creation. In my mind's eye, I began to levitate. The message continued:

> *Levitation is experienced with unity with all there is. Rise above the petty things day-to-day life brings you. Allow your true self to step to the forefront. Acknowledge and honor your connection*

to all. Bring inspiration through your heart, your sacred, silent heart, for it is within the quiet energy of love that all will be healed.

The experience made me realize my true essence was nonphysical. I am not my body. I am not the human structure that I drag out of bed each morning. My true self is my spirit, my soul; it's nonphysical.

No matter what aches and pains I experience, nothing can destroy the true me; it lives on. I am pure energy, and I can use that energy to travel to the upper realms where I can feel the unity of all that is. That is my real home, not this beautiful planet where I've lived for six decades.

The first of the six Seraphim Blueprint classes had connected me with the seraphim who remain a part of my life. It's easy to recognize their presence. When purple colors flow through my mind's eye, I know they surround me and are ready to speak. They connected with me during the five remaining classes, but sometimes they surprised me by showing up when I least expected.

Five months after my first Seraphim Blueprint class, I attended another one. It was the first Saturday of the winter break, and I couldn't think of a better way to start the holidays. It felt like the gang was back together again as Maria, Scott, and I met with Gigi to continue our trek into the realm of the seraphim.

The energies during the first activation were intense as I swam in the shapeless moments that exist between sleep and wakefulness. It was the magical space of the nonphysical. Within moments, I popped out of my current existence to enter the Realms of Light. This is a nonphysical area I had visited several years before. It is a place where many ascended masters reside. I took a deep breath, welcoming the following words into my awareness:

December 19, 2015

I am spirit. I am light. I am one with all, all that there is. I am not of the Earth plane but of the gentle blanket of feathers, keeping me tethered and grounded. My true essence is love, and my truth is light.

With each breath, I am peace. I am light. I am love. I am all there is.

While floating blissfully in a ray of purple mist, I knew the seraphim had returned. Slipping from the density of Earth and drifting toward the spiritual realms, I took a quick inventory of my surroundings. As our blue-green planet dropped from view, a trail of sparks followed me, releasing a shower of golden flecks against the deep blue painted atmosphere. I finally understood this was me—I was divine light.

With that realization, I wondered about the message. Had it been from the angels, or had I spoken through the messenger?

As I drew closer to the source of my true nature, I drifted into a delicious pause of serenity and peace. I smiled when I realized my connection to the seraphim had allowed these experiences. The message continued:

It is the luminescence of the moon, the divine energy from the feminine that enters you, enters your essence, your light. It is soft, yet strong in its connection and its reflection. The moon is a reflection of source, as you are a reflection of the power, strength, and divine love of all that is. Wear it. Wear it well. Let your essence reflect the power, strength, and love of the divine source of all, the power of the angels.

Seraphim frequencies entered my heart, and in my mind's eye, I saw a swirling vortex of violet, lilac, and lavender colors.

Looking like a spider's web, this whirlpool of spinning silk moved to the bottoms of my feet.

The energy on my soles was intense, and I reached to rub them. The colorful webbed matrix moved from beneath my feet upward until it had encapsulated my entire body. Like a leaf captured in a wind-blown spider's web, I was suspended, balanced in the dimension between the divine and Earth. A thought entered my awareness, and I intuitively knew this was a lesson about the importance of staying grounded when connected to spiritual realms. The message continued:

There is a connection with all there is. It is the heart center that is the intelligence behind all human interaction and all human emotions. Know of your heart's link to all there is; know that as you give energy and attention to something, you give of yourself, for this is your vibratory signature. It goes with you. It is an electrical current signature of your heart. Keep a balance. As within, so without. As above, so below.

It felt so real to gently sway in midair, bound between Earth and the higher dimensions by the seraphim's silky purple webbing. I realized this vision had captured the essence of the opening message, describing me as spirit, light, and love. I existed neither in Earth nor spiritual realms; I was tethered between these two dimensions.

Our hearts connect us to everything, maintaining equilibrium between within and without as well as balancing aspects of above and below. If I used my heart, I could tap into higher vibrations. If I remained firmly grounded, I'd be in the perfect position to use this divine discernment in my everyday life.

As we evolve and connect with higher realms, we keep the energy flowing in both directions. We are suspended between dimensions, bridging the gap as we usher higher vibrational frequencies back to Earth. We are those connections. I was so thankful to the seraphim for their clarity and guidance.

Four months later, I questioned whether I would make it to the end of the school year. The only thing that kept me going was counting the days until summer break. Working as a school psychologist was demanding, but the upcoming two-month recess made it all worthwhile.

It was an April weekend, and after placing my empty coffee cup in the sink, I decided to take an early-morning jog. I donned my long-sleeved sun shirt, grabbed my water and hat, and headed to the car. It was seven in the morning, and I wanted to take advantage of the relatively low humidity and the seventy-eight-degree temperature. There are a couple of nature trails close to my home, and I hoped to get there before it got any warmer.

The eight-minute drive to the Gordon River Greenway was quiet. I pulled into the nearly empty parking lot as the sun peeked above the horizon. I shoved my purse under the front seat, secured my sunhat, attached earbuds to my phone, started my fitness watch, and took off at a leisurely jog. It wasn't long before I veered off the paved path toward a large clump of dew-clung grasses, and the familiar tug of a messenger entered my awareness. I took a deep breath, and within that meditative pause, I found myself immersed in a veil of purple mist; the seraphim were here. I opened my phone's voice recorder and captured the following:

April 16, 2016

It matters not whether you feel or sense this, for it is real, it is true. Our energies are subtle, for we are of the subtle realms. We are as a gentle breeze that sways the blossoms of flowers and enlivens them.

I was surprised when the figure of Mother Mary appeared in

my mind's eye. She was holding an egg-shaped gem. Although its color reminded me of amethyst, for reasons I cannot explain, I knew it was a purple sapphire.

She held it high above her head as if offering it to the Creator. In response, a stream of light entered the top of the gemstone egg, spotlighting Mother Mary in a shower of deep lavender. I looked around in surprise when I realized the purple light had also cast its glow over me. The message continued:

It is the allowing of the energy to flow which starts this initiation process. Just as life begins with an egg, this egg represents the onset of initiation. This is an energy gift to you, the beginning of a journey, your new journey in life. Your path has changed. These divine energies have altered it.

I knew the message referred to the initiations I had received through Seraphim Blueprint; I was halfway through the six classes. As the words entered my awareness, the angels sent a picture of a white dandelion seed head ready to release its seeds into the air. The message continued:

The energy is as pure and gentle as the tender breeze that blows the dandelion seed head but only bending the individual seeds. The seeds remain intact. They do not take flight.

The energy is as gentle and slow as a wave in the center of the ocean, swelling and falling but not cresting. It is as if the sea herself is taking a deep breath.

I continued my jog, but the boundaries of my physical body disintegrated. I couldn't feel my feet as they landed on the mulched path. I dissolved, becoming one with all. As if on cue, the messenger described what I was experiencing:

Go within to find that connection to the light. For when you do so, all of those parameters and boundaries you thought were there will magically disappear.

Go within to find the truth. There are no boundaries. Nothing is preventing your travels. Go, go, go, my friend. Go to wherever your heart desires, for it is your heart that leads the way.

Within seconds, I felt my essence leave my body, and the divine light of creation itself permeated me. Two short sentences began looping within my mind like a never-ending mantra: "I am one with all. I am all that I am."

As the chant echoed in the background, I had a vision of a stone dropping in the center of a body of calm water. The farther the rock fell, the larger the waves became.

I understood what this meant. As we connect with the higher vibrations of angels, we create a ripple effect on our planet. We bring forth these divine energies into our daily lives, enriching us beyond measure. It's not just for us, we elevate those within our wake.

The vision and messages ended as quickly as they had begun. I continued my run, crossing the tall pedestrian bridge over the Gordon River. By the time I returned to my car, the temperature was in the mid-eighties, and the humidity was stifling.

I started the engine and cranked the air conditioner to full blast. I wiped my dripping brow and neck with a towel, and after several long gulps of water, I headed home. I couldn't help but smile at my unexpected encounter with the seraphim on my morning run. I'm sure other walkers and joggers have great adventures on the Gordon River Greenway, but I'm guessing mine was unique.

The following month, I attended another Seraphim Blueprint class that brought me to another level of understanding of these angelic beings. As usual, the purple mist accompanied the seraphim, and significant energy flowed during the initiations, but something was different, very different. A new and personal connection emerged when I came face-to-face with an angel who introduced himself as "The Seraph."

When I first saw him, his power and compassion overwhelmed me. My heart pounded, and my palms were wet as I tried, unsuccessfully, to squeeze back the tears. Like water bursting through a dam, I sobbed uncontrollably, raining tears on my journal. Finally, my heart slowed its rapid beating, and my hands stopped shaking enough for me to write my experiences.

The Seraph was high in the atmosphere, hovering above our blue-green planet. The surrounding purple of deep space wafted through his translucent body. He pointed one of his enormous wings upward while the other reached toward Earth.

The tips of his wings released a purple vapor, ablaze with golden sparks of light. He began to move upward, spiraling in slow motion. As he rotated, the glittering purple mist swirled from each wing, creating two mirror-imaged vortices. I could only see the mouth of the upper funnel, but I had a better view of its lower counterpart as its glittering trail fell in silent circles below, covering our planet.

With a wistful eye, I surveyed The Seraph's upward trajectory in the center of the tunnel above him. My heart ached when I realized he was moving through these other-dimensional spaces toward his home. He was leaving, yet he had left behind the gold-filled rings of mist that continued to layer our Earth. As he departed, he spoke the following:

May 28, 2016

Trust. Know that you are protected. Allow the flow. Believe what you see.

My communications with the seraphim had begun with the dream the year before, and I had become accustomed to their energy, but this was different. It was more personal and many times more powerful.

This intimate contact also held universal implications. The glittering rings emanating from this mighty angel encircled the Earth, and I understood their protective nature. The Seraph was sending energy to our beloved planet, helping to safeguard and heal her.

Gratitude swelled within me as I thought of my experience of meeting The Seraph. I was so thankful, yet my heart ached when I saw him leave. Soon I learned this would not be our final farewell.

Almost three months later, I gathered my belongings and headed to Sandra McGill's house for the final chapter of Seraphim Blueprint. Lots of changes had occurred since my initial class. Gigi had moved to Brazil, and I was back where I had begun. Returning to Sandra's had brought me full circle.

I reflected on this program that had been such an essential aspect of my life; it was difficult to believe it was coming to a halt. The day sped past and as the evening approached, I had a vision. All of the seraphim frequencies I had received over the past thirteen months combined in front of my eyes, embodied as a gold chain.

The chain floated in midair, set against a backdrop of what I had come to know as the seraphim's signature: deep purple mist. There were eleven links, each representing a seraphim energy. The two end pieces drifted toward each other and connected, transforming the chain into what appeared to be a necklace.

It began spinning in a clockwise direction, picking up speed with each second. Soon, the whirl of individual links morphed into an unbroken loop of gold. It moved from its midair position, gliding upward until it hovered above the head of The Seraph, who, to my surprise, had just entered. The chain of seraphim energies had become his halo.

The vision was a perfect ending to the Seraphim Blueprint classes, and a sense of satisfaction swept through me. I was ready to close this precious chapter of my life and file it in a place I could readily access. I had watched The Seraph with his Seraphim Blueprint activated halo, and having swapped my awe for contentment, I felt complete. Now, I thought, I am prepared to leave, but The Seraph had another message. He spoke one statement, a sentence that shined a light on years of memories:

August 21, 2016

We brought your beloved home.

I gasped in disbelief. That one sentence confirmed, in retrospect, what should have been obvious: the seraphim had escorted my husband into the afterlife. Almost thirty years had passed since I had seen the winged-footed angels who were in human disguise.

As far back as 1987, the seraphim had orchestrated bits and pieces of my life, and finally, they shared their secret. I thought of all the boxes that had been checked for this to occur—angels in a hospital waiting room, dreams of the healing powers of seraphim, multiple messages, and Seraphim Blueprint classes.

Since my opening to spirit in 2013, I felt as if a curtain had lifted, granting me access to a world unseen by most. My destiny unfolded within the subtle play and patterns of synchronicity, and long ago, I had learned better than to discount something just because I couldn't prove it.

I smiled with the recognition that The Seraph's statement solved a mystery that had shrouded my life for almost thirty years. A deep sense of indebtedness rose from within as I gave my heartfelt thanks for this information.

More now than ever before, I understand life is a puzzle full of clues, and so often, we see the world but miss the details. The Seraph had provided clarity, and those specifics added an incredible layer of understanding.

A pattern emerged, one filled with hope, comfort, tenderness, and love. It's true. The seraphim had been with Daryl in his time of need. They were his companions on his final transition, yet they had first come to me. I had seen them in the hospital's waiting room, and an hour later, they had reappeared through the words of the hospital chaplain as he asked for the angels with winged feet to carry Daryl home.

These divine beings had accompanied my husband into the afterlife, yet I now understand one very important message—they never left. They remained here for me.

I began to see the larger picture. Angels are our guiding lights, ever-present, ready to answer our pleas for help, contacting us in the subtleties of everyday life, always willing to assist. I invite you to turn inward and contemplate these divine beings. Call on them in your time of need and know they never leave your side. Learn to toss your anchor past the physical senses into a deeper truth, the intangible world of the seraphim.

CHAPTER 7: EARTH ANGELS

I t happened so fast. Just moments before, I was walking down a meandering path, simply enjoying nature. How did I get here? For a brief moment, I thought I was dreaming.

A shimmering veil of energy covered my body like dawn's thin mist. I ran my hands over my damp forearms. Yes, the drizzle is real, I thought, as I continued walking this path that had changed in front of my eyes. I was still here, but everything else was different.

What cosmic doorway had I entered? Where was I? Little did I know I had crossed the threshold into another dimensional space, one that was sacred and blessed.

This scene took place in early November 2018. Although temperatures were usually cooler this time of year, the thermometer approached eighty as I began a morning walk in a nearby community park. The scenic Gordon River Greenway is a perfect place for communing with nature, precisely what I needed. It was Sunday morning; I smiled when I realized my retirement five months before allowed these walks any weekday, no longer just on weekends.

After a more than forty-year career as a psychologist, taking down my shingle eliminated the 4:40 a.m. alarms. I had published

The Reluctant Messenger~Tales from Beyond Belief a few weeks after retirement, but now what? As I searched for balance in my new-found freedom, I realized these morning nature walks offered an ideal transition to life as a happy retiree.

I veered off the paved trail, seeking a deeper connection to the woods, and that's when I felt a discernible vibrational shift. It surprised me; these changes in my energy field usually occurred during meditations, not woodland walks.

A sense of timelessness prevailed as I turned in the direction of a mockingbird's melodious song. Had it been there before? A gentle breeze cooled the back of my neck and scalp near the base of my ponytail. I took a deep breath, inhaling the musky scent of nearby pines. I looked around and marveled at the swirling patterns of dappled sunlight as it pierced the verdant leaves above.

The sights and sounds were too vivid for a dream, and it was more vibrant than my normal waking state. All my senses were on high alert, yet a wave of serenity and tranquility washed over me. I wanted to absorb this peace; I had to.

I sat to remove my socks and tennis shoes; for some reason, I needed to feel the soil beneath my feet. I had no desire to stand, so I surrendered to the moment and stretched out on the damp ground. I rested my head on the soft mulch; the sun's rays danced across my body through the filter of branches above. I caught a whiff of the sweet fragrance of jasmine.

I succumbed to this profound force that called me from deep within Earth's core. White clouds drifted in a sea of blue above as I closed my eyes and faded into these delicious frequencies that summoned my soul.

I have no idea how much time passed, but an understanding swept into my awareness, and I knew what had happened. I had passed through an interdimensional doorway to a sacred realm; I was in the space where angels dwell.

November 4, 2018

Look around for we are here. We are part of all there is, and our presence surrounds humans upon this Earth. Our energies have been with you since before your human incarnation. We shall be with you as you exit this life and embrace another form.

The messengers were angels. As this information came into my awareness, I looked around. I had stepped into a space outside my current existence, and I wanted to savor this moment.

After several deep breaths, I sat, then rose to my feet. I looked around. Everything moved in slow motion, from the lavender-tipped leaves of a nearby clump of tall grass as it swayed in the morning breeze to the movement of my head as I scanned the surroundings. I saw nothing but perfection.

I understood I existed as part of this divine plan. I felt connected to nature in a way I never had before. The plants and trees felt like family, and I realized they were as much alive as I was. They were sentient, conscious beings.

I had walked this path before, past this almost immeasurable beauty. How could I not have noticed it? This day everything was different; I had become part of the nature surrounding me.

An orange butterfly flitted so close that I ducked to avoid colliding with it. As I swerved, a beautiful blanket of tiny yellow and purple flowers caught my attention. I realized my connection to the angels had brought me a greater realization of this beauty that I had not noticed, much less appreciated. While admiring this exquisiteness, the angels continued:

As with all energy forms, we, too, have different levels that correspond to frequencies. Some of us are more closely tied to natural phenomena in the Earth plane—nature. Humans have sometimes called us fairies, but we are of the angelic realm.

117

We are Earth angels. As we surround various flowers, plants, trees, etc., we aid in the growth and development of that specific species.

Are fairies Earth angels? I smiled at this surprising discovery. I thought about my fascination with the fairies. Not only had I believed in them as a child, I continue to do so.

My long-standing fondness for these diminutive winged beings is apparent in my home. Several years ago, two artists from Canada transformed my half-bath into an enchanted woodland scene—a perfect home for my fairy friends.

Stu and Vi hung a print of Edward Robert Hughes' painting, *Midsummer Eve,* in the center of the room.[10] This early 1900s picture of a young woman in a forest surrounded by light-bearing fairies serves as a focal point. With deft skills that matched the original, these talented artists continued Hughes' masterpiece. The scene spills over the frame and onto the walls to create an enchanted forest home for my fairy friends.

A beautiful tree-shaped Tiffany lamp provides soft lighting for the small fairy figurines suspended from deep-green vines framing a mirrored wall. The lamp shade's multicolored wisteria stained-glass leaves cast a mystical glow on *Midsummer Eve,* bringing it to life.

I felt joyous to learn the fairies were part of the angel realm. Although I had never thought of them as Earth angels, they were the logical angelic candidates to serve as nature's protectors. The message continued:

Humans are sometimes surprised to see a small plant that grows in an unlikely environment such as a boulder, asphalt, slab of concrete, or any other material that would appear to be

10 https://www.the-athenaeum.org/art/detail.php?ID=117869

uninhabitable, a place that does not appear to be optimal for growth. Yet within the confines of this harsh environment, life has found its way, and the plant thrives.

We say to you that this ability to thrive in such conditions is due in part to the intervention of the Earth angels, the fairies. It is their protection and nurturing and care that allows the seemingly impossible to become possible. Such is the power of the angels.

As humans continue to evolve in consciousness, the veil separating our dimensions begins to dissipate, and then our presence becomes known.

Once humans acknowledge our presence, it becomes easier for them to call on us in a time of need. Their eyes begin to open, and they learn to perceive with a new set of eyes. They see more than what they were cable of before. Beauty abounds, yet it takes a sense of stillness and an attitude of wonder to begin to appreciate these experiences in their fullness.

The description resonated with me. I had veered off the paved path and entered another dimensional space. I passed through a mysterious veil that awakened me to the beauty and life that surrounded me. It had always been there, but I had not noticed until this day. The message continued:

There is a new breed of humans coming to the Earth plane. These children have awakened, much more so than previous generations. This is part of the evolution of humankind. It is this new breed of children who will work more directly with us in the angel realm. They will not only recognize our guidance, but they will actively seek answers to problems in the Earth plane by collaboration with us.

There is much rejoicing and jubilation from the angel realm, for this new breed of children represents hope. Their priorities will become more consciously driven, no longer directed by personality or ego. There is wisdom behind their thoughts and actions as we provide knowledge and guidance. Embrace this new change, for it is the light that will guide those in the Earth plane to wisdom. This is all for now.

As the message ended, I took another deep breath and looked around. The sparkling surroundings faded like a brief shower on a hot summer sidewalk, leaving me in the woodland's silence. The enchantment took wing, revealing the old world I'd left behind, but that, too, was different. I could no longer know this place as I had before.

I remembered a quote from W. B. Yeats about the magic that's in this world, and how it quietly waited for us to be able to sense it. Had my explorations through the veil renewed my senses? I only hoped I would retain some of the magic I had experienced.

I returned to the Greenway the next morning, hoping to reconnect with these divine beings. As I exited my car and walked toward the park's boardwalk, they began to speak. I turned on my phone and recorded the following:

November 5, 2018

Feel the connection. From deep within Mother Earth, tendrils reach up to the ethers, guided by the spirit of Mother Earth. For you see, her energies are in tune with the manifestation of her spirit. She is the heart of Earth, and this is how Earth angels are guided.

A vivid image formed in my mind's eye, and I felt myself becoming progressively smaller until I was the size of a pea. The shrinking-woman me looked up from inside a transparent bubble.

Was this a drop of dew?

I was in two places simultaneously. There was the physical me who walked the Greenway and the me within the vision. As I viewed the world through the lens of this transparent globe, the clarity took my breath away. It was beyond what my physical eyes were capable of seeing.

Morning dew clung to the tips of pine needles, shimmering in the fresh light from the morning sun. My eyes shifted to a spider's web; its intricate, delicate threads lazily drifted in the morning breeze. These almost-invisible filaments glided in the up and down rhythmic movement of lungs, taking deep breaths. Tears spilled down my cheeks as I marveled at the splendor.

I bent down for a closer look at a small single-stemmed pink flower of a sunshine mimosa plant. The detail seemed to unfold as I got closer; its white-tipped lavender points that surrounded a deep red center appeared to float in the morning breeze.

As I studied the blossom, I felt another shift as my consciousness dropped into the flower. Still confined within the center of the transparent orb, I became small enough to fit between the plant's tiny velvety spikes in the center of the bloom. I continued to shrink until I was the size of a grain of sand.

Although I knew this occurred in my mind's eye, it did not detract from the sensation that I was actually inside the plant. Over the years, I'd grown accustomed to visions, but this was more detailed and realistic than others. I wondered why this experience was different.

When I thought the strange could not get stranger, it did. The small aspect of myself split into two particles. One traveled up the stem while the other went into the root system. I moved upward toward the sun, beckoning its life-sustaining rays for photosynthesis. I reached down through the roots for stability and to gather nutrients from the fertile soil. Traveling within the bubble of energy had allowed me to perceive the world differently, and

I felt connected to nature in a way I had never experienced. For a brief period, I had become a flower. I wondered if this was how the Earth angels worked.

I finished my hike and headed to the car. As I packed my gear into the trunk, I knew I had returned to the world of form. A sense of déjà vu washed over me, catapulting me to the day of my first message in August 2013. Had I just become the flower—that flow-er of energy connecting Father Sky to Mother Earth from my initial message?

My spiritual journey had led me far from my beginnings, and I realized this was a result of learning a new way of seeing. What was real? I understand the world of physicality, but the rich world of energy was beginning to feel more genuine than my day-to-day living, and that wasn't such a bad thing.

Nine days later, I was sitting on my balcony, sipping a cup of coffee. It was an early Wednesday morning, and I opted for relaxing instead of a brisk morning walk. Nothing was on the agenda until early afternoon when I would need to pick up Shalane from her prekindergarten class.

As I sipped my hot brew, I thought about the most recent experiences with my cosmic friends. I'd had several communications but none with the Earth angels. I couldn't stop thinking about them; it had been more than a week since the last contact. These thoughts must have called them to my awareness, for within moments, the following arrived:

November 14, 2018

There are many names for Earth angels, such as fairies, but there are also other such elementals. They are part of the heavenly realm, and they are tasked with protecting nature on the Earth plane. The spirit of Mother Earth guides them. In conjunction with the heavenly realms, this subset of angels oversees the

122

natural phenomena on your most divine planet. Other subsets help with more cosmic surroundings, but that is not for the discussion today.

We guide the spirit of Mother Earth, Gaia, and she, in turn, translates our guidance into energy frequencies that direct these tiny, powerful Earth angels. Some humans have seen these beings with their eyes, but that is not yet a common Earthly phenomenon.

Earth angels can be felt and sensed by sensitive humans. Their presence can sometimes be captured by electronic means, although most often, they present as a wisp or ball of energy.

Capturing their presence by electronic means? My mind went back to June 2016. I was attending a program at Monroe Institute when I met Fatima from Brazil, who had seen a photograph of a real fairy. Fatima's physician's husband had taken the picture while at a remote camping lodge in Brazil.

I remember when Fatima handed me her phone to show me the picture of this photograph. There it was, a tiny figure resting on a small branch arching over the edge of a body of water. It looked like an attractive young woman in pale green clothing with shoulder-length light brown hair, but her tiny size and wings suggested she was anything but ordinary. I could see the fairy's face, arms, and pale blue wings that faded to off-white near the tips.

As I typed the summary of Fatima's story in the book draft, I remembered reading a passage that had described another fairy sighting. I pulled *The Wheel of Life* from the oversized bookshelf in my bedroom and quickly found it: medical doctor Elisabeth Kubler-Ross' story that paralleled Fatima's account.

I searched online for the back story. In John Harricharan's interview, entitled *A Conversation with Dr. Elisabeth Kubler-Ross,*

Kubler-Ross described meeting a woman in Virginia who had the uncanny ability to photograph garden fairies.[11] The woman gave Dr. Kubler-Ross a photo of a flower. Upon closer look, perched on the plant was a "creature with a small body, face, and wings."

To prove the picture was genuine, the Virginia woman retrieved a Polaroid camera, handed it to her guest, and led Dr. Kubler-Ross to the garden. Dr. Kubler-Ross focused on a flower and snapped the shutter. The camera's rollers ejected the negative, and within seconds, the picture began to develop. Dr. Kubler-Ross, too, had photographed a fairy!

Re-reading Dr. Kubler-Ross' story reminded me of an October 2013 communication where the messengers foretold that people would begin to see fairy folk and other-dimensional beings. Experiencing fairies, gnomes, and sprites is part of Earth's expansion to a higher vibrational state. As people's foundational beliefs begin to crack, it makes room for the newer energies for Gaia's evolution.

Is this what is happening now? More people's perspectives stretch to comprehend what was once thought to be impossible. Before August 2013, I would have never guessed I'd have intimate connections to angels and other messengers of light, yet here I am.

A couple of days later, I drove to Goddess I Am for Friday's morning meditation. A few minutes before it was to begin, store owner, Beth Brown-Rinella, entered through the back door. Something caught her attention in the canal that separates the building from a residential community. She thought she had seen a manatee, a slow-moving sea mammal that often seeks warmer inland waters when the weather cools.

Beth walked to the front of the store where several of us waited outside, bundled in our sweaters and light jackets for these mid-November temperatures. She unlocked the doors with an

---

11 http://www.insight2000.com/kubler-ross.html

invitation to join her search for the often-elusive manatee.

We meandered between tables filled with crystals, incense, and statues of various metaphysical icons and angels until we reached the back of the store. Something was new. In the center of the meditation room stood a four-foot-tall copper frame of a pyramid. We moved around its perimeter and stepped outside through the back door.

The cold temperatures met us—another reminder winter was approaching. I walked to the edge of the canal and stood for a few minutes, but the breeze sent shivers down my spine. Soon I joined the others in a quick retreat to the warmth of the shop.

But we were no longer alone when we entered the building; something had joined us. As Beth opened the heavy metal door, she created a vacuum that pulled swift-moving energy into the room. I didn't know what it was, but I knew this nonphysical phenomenon would make itself known in due time.

The meditation would begin shortly, so I settled into my chair and removed my light jacket that rarely gets used in this subtropical climate. As I retrieved my pen and journal, I felt the presence of a large, sprawling oak tree.

Its full canopy engulfed the interior and exterior of the building where Goddess I Am is located. I intuitively knew the tree served as a safe haven. I knew it protected the people inside Goddess I Am, but there was more. I understood this gigantic oak provided a place of refuge for the unknown energy that had entered through the back door of the shop.

I smiled as I recognized the new visitors: Earth angels. The fairies had returned. The message began:

November 16, 2018

As your beloved planet continues in her transition to a more spiritual nature, so are all her inhabitants, including elementals.

They, too, are stepping into their divine nature.

My perspective zoomed to above the building's green tin roof. I saw a flurry of activity from the water, shrubs, trees, and flowers bordering the canal. Fairies! All at once, they swarmed toward the back entrance of Goddess I Am. Their swift flight abruptly ended, creating a cluster of fairies at the threshold. After a brief pause, they adeptly slipped beneath the doorway, entering our meditation space.

My point of view changed again, and I found myself snuggled in my chair, journaling the vision. I glanced at the back wall; clouds of fairies continued to sweep beneath the closed door. They entered and roosted in the branches of the giant oak tree that had materialize only moments before.

These fairies were busy, flitting from branch to branch as if searching for the best spot to land. With each perch change, the tree became more vibrant. Was the energy from the Earth angels awakening the life force within the tree?

Without warning, the swarm darted from the lower branches to settle on top of the tree's canopy. They danced and fluttered for several seconds before they quieted, appearing contented to relax on the tree's upper branches.

Other people came for the meditation, and when the final participant arrived, as if on cue, the Earth angels descended. They swooped and swirled, weaving brilliant, golden streams of energy around us, creating loosely woven cocoons.

The observer-me watched the busy Earth angels as they continued wrapping us in their mystical threads. When my cocoon became solid, I experienced a shift in consciousness. I found myself nestled deep within the womb of the gilded orb. I felt suspended in time and space, surrounded by immeasurable peace and serenity.

I heard and felt a rumbling from the bowels of Earth, and within seconds, a tidal wave engulfed the room. The deluge permeated our surroundings, yet we remained blissful in the muted silence of our golden orbs.

A few moments before the meditation had begun, Beth had shaken a shaman's rattle around each participant to loosen errant energy fragments. As I watched the flood from my mind's eye, I realized these waters were cleansing and clearing those stray energies that had been released by Beth's actions with the rattle. After several minutes, water rushed upward, through the apex of the copper pyramid in the center of the room.

As the last vestiges of water trickled from our meditation area, the fairies began the task of unwrapping our cocoons. We were different. We had transformed like butterflies emerging from chrysalises. As we stepped into the world anew, I had a vision.

In my mind's eye, Venus emerged from the sea, riding on a half shell. Once she reached land, the seashell morphed into a lotus flower, and she transformed into a wisp of smoke that disappeared into the cosmos.

I couldn't stop the rush of tears as I grasped the meaning of the vision. The understanding was much larger than words could describe. Venus represented us. She emerged through the four elements of Earth to transform to her true nature—divine unity. We are part of all that is, connected to everything in the cosmos and beyond.

Our divine unity is one of the hallmark themes from the messengers, and to have it repeated during this morning meditation brought its significance to the forefront. Understanding our connection to all that is adds clarity to our minds, and that can light the way for others. Once again, I felt humbled to be in the presence of such wisdom.

Once home, I decided to investigate my vision of Venus. Research revealed Italian Renaissance artist Sandro painted *The*

Birth of Venus in approximately 1484.[12] The painting depicts the goddess Venus arriving to shore on a half shell after being birthed from the sea, full-grown.

I compared these findings with the meditation experience. Like Venus, we had been rebirthed from water when the fairies unwrapped our golden orbs. We, too, had emerged full-grown and transformed. Yet there was more: Venus had morphed into a goddess, and so had we. After all, our experiences had begun as we entered the front doors of the shop aptly named Goddess I Am.

The following Friday morning, I returned to Goddess I Am. I pulled into the parking lot, gathered my journal, water, purse, and headed inside. I was not alone; the gentle flutters of the Earth angels surrounded me. While Beth prepared the room for the meditation, I joined the others and quickly took a seat in time to record the following message:

November 23, 2018

It is all about the yin and yang, the checks and balances, that fine line between trust and fear. Learn to walk your path with the eyes of the heart, for your heart will never lead you astray. Trust that each step on that path takes you in the direction of the divine, even though your physical eyes may not comprehend.

Trust your heart.

A fountain of red water gushed to life in the center of the room. Droplets broke away and created a mist that permeated the surroundings. The spray began to take form, and I smiled as these minuscule droplets morphed into fairies.

These Earth angels buzzed around each of us, creating gentle vibrations throughout our bodies. They zipped in and out, up and down, in a flight path reminiscent of hummingbirds. I laughed at

---

12 https://g.co/arts/PM89DPXjKyrxTeZL9

my first instinct to swat at them as they flew close to my head. As I watched the dance of the swarming fairies, an angel spoke:

We give these Earth angels the powers of healing. Just as they provide sustenance to plants and animals upon your planet, they also surround humans with these powerful vibrations. They assist in the balance of nature with their interactions.

As I scribbled these words in my journal, I noticed movement from above as waves of energy descended. My breath quickened, and tears formed in my eyes when I recognized Archangel Raphael. He took a deep breath and exhaled through his mouth. I intuitively knew he was infusing the room with life-force energy through prana, the breath of life.

His breath permeated the air, causing ash-like particles of energy to lift from our bodies. It was only then I understood the purpose of the Earth angels. Similar to Beth's shaman rattle from the previous week, the vibrations from the fairy fly-bys had loosened low-vibrational energy, clearing the way for Raphael's breath of life. It was out with the old, in with the new.

These deep healing vibrations rendered me speechless, and when the time came for me to share my experience, I did so with a lump in my throat. When the meditation ended, I gathered my belongings and walked to the car, thinking about my experiences. I realized I felt different. This encounter had humbled me, and I felt honored to have been witness to the events, but it was more than that. On some level, I understood these angelic frequencies had long-lasting healing implications that I would feel for years to come.

Several weeks later, on a whim, I decided to search for more information on Raphael. I shook my head in disbelief when I learned the word Raphael means "God has healed."[13]

I tried to absorb this new information about Earth angels. Now that I know fairies are part of the angelic realm, would this changed perspective alter the meaning of previous messages? With my curiosity piqued, I opened my online journal and searched for more information on fairies and angels. I found detailed notes from a Seraphim Blueprint angel class led by Gigi Petersen in 2016.

Gigi was a gifted psychic whose specialty was channeling angels, but I soon discovered she could speak with fairies. Reviewing my journal catapulted me back to that day in September 2016.

Maria, my friend who often accompanies me on spiritual adventures, hosted the class at her house. During a break, we strolled around her spacious yard. It was an ideal time to introduce Gigi to the guardian who protects Maria's home.

A couple of years before, Maria had bought a metal Dollar Tree garden stake in the shape of a garden angel, a fairy. She had secured the figurine's deep footing in a large planter adjacent to her front door. One day, the garden angel disappeared, gone without a trace.

Several weeks later, as I walked with Maria down her winding driveway to check her mailbox, I felt the presence of a messenger. I was on high alert. As Maria gathered her mail, I heard "Look up."

There was Maria's Dollar Tree fairy, gracefully entwined in electrical lines on top of a thirty-five-foot utility pole. We marveled at how this could have happened. The figurine was made from a thin sheet of metal, much too light to toss that distance. How had this happened?

When Maria finished sharing the story with Gigi, we had reached the property's edge; she pointed to the fairy who, two years later, remained on top of the utility pole. As we walked back

13 http://www.newadvent.org/cathen/12640b.htm

to the house through the tree-lined driveway, mid-conversation Gigi said, "White is part of her name." I knew Gigi channeled angels, but I didn't expect her to communicate with a metal figurine bought at Dollar Tree.

We entered the house and made ourselves comfortable to begin the second half of the class. As soon as I sat down, a message poured into my awareness:

September 25, 2016

I am called Lily White, and I represent the protective energy of the angelic realm as well as the energy of the Earthly realm. Many refer to me as an Earth angel, for I spend the majority of my time protecting the ones I love on the Earth plane.

I have given my energy to protect the property and those who live here. I surround them with love and protection, not only here, but when they venture into the world.

In my mind's eye, I saw Lily from a bird's-eye perspective. Although in three-dimensional reality she was a metal figurine from Dollar Tree, her energy body floated outside her metal form entwined in the powerlines. Beautiful white light radiated from her chest and scanned the property like a lighthouse's powerful beam. But it wasn't just light; she emitted a thin protective mist that soon covered the house and yard. The message continued:

When you leave the property, you are covered, much like walking through a spider's web. You drag the energy with you, and it encompasses you. You are enfolded in its protective shield. When you return, the frequencies pull at your energy body, cleansing you, purifying you. Believe. Allow. Accept. Give thanks.

My intentions are as pure as the lilies of the field, the lilies of the valley. My intentions are as pure as a snowdrop upon a blanket of white snow.

My heart is pure. I surround you with love and peace. Let the light of my heart burn through your body, dissolving any negativity, transmuting negative energy into positive.

A vision began. From a panoramic view from above, I saw hundreds of tiny floating sparks landing on grasses, flowers, and trees. It was a few seconds before I realized these glimmers of light were fairies. A message accompanied the vision:

When invited, we sometimes hide within a drop of dew by blending with our sister water sprites. As our golden lights merge, it creates an iridescent shimmer. This provides us with nourishment and a place of comfort as we hide from Earthly eyes.

We settle into the plants and all the flora of the land, melting into the energy frequency. We become the powerhouse of the plant, releasing and realigning energy transfers to promote optimal growth.

We are the flowers, the flow-ers.

As they spoke this last sentence, I heard a discernable giggle. I understood the reference to my very first message in August 2013, about people being flow-ers of energy. The message continued:

We are what enlivens the plants. We help with the absorption rate to maximize photosynthesis to a level of perfection. There is another set of elementals who do the same for the animal and mineral kingdoms.

Then, with a melody so pronounced I could almost hear it with my physical ears, the fairies sang the following:

Open your heart, and your ears will hear. Open your heart, and your eyes will see. Open your heart and sing and dance with us.

Chills darted up and down my spine, and a tear sprang from my eye and splashed onto my journal as I penned these words. The angels blanketed me in waves of love and protection. The message continued:

Rest, Sweet One, accept these sacred, nourishing energies. Breathe in the sweetness, breathe in the life force. Be one with us. Play with us as we flitter about the universe, sprinkling our love and laughter throughout the woodlands, the mountains, the fields of flowers, calling humanity to fly with us.

As I smiled at the message, a mass of energy materialized and hovered a few feet away. This swirl took shape; I realized I was face-to-face with myself. As the cloud-of-energy me turned to make a midair exit, I laughed at the sight of gossamer wings that propelled me into the sky. The me seated at the meditation beamed with delight as I realized an aspect of myself had accepted the fairies' invitation to play.

I revisited this 2016 experience, and I realized Lily had not only initiated the messages from the fairies, but she had introduced the concept of Earth angels. I now understand why I had been guided to review this older experience. The concept of Earth angels was not a new perspective, just a forgotten one. These nonphysical entities unite Earth with the higher vibrational fields from the nonphysical. They are the perfect connection between these two dimensions.

A grin spread across my face as I relived the fairies' 2016 invitation for me to play. It reminded me of my grandchildren, Lorelai and Shalane, and the hours we have spent playing together. There is such a profound innocence to children at play—

no worries, no bother, only laughter, imagination, and exploration.

Perhaps that is the lesson from the Earth angels. Learn to release that which does not serve you. Don't fret about things you cannot change. Go with the flow, be the flow-er of that radiant energy of life. Allow it to stream through your existence to connect to the higher vibrational frequencies of the angels.

Yes, perhaps it is time to play. In response to my new understanding, the messengers spoke:

September 22, 2019

Be ye like the animals that inhabit your Earth. Learn to live among the natural elements. Learn to live from within your heart center. When you are tethered to the heart of Gaia, you have free rein to soar among her inhabitants safely.

Go and explore, for we shall guide and protect you. We give you the means to soar and reach toward Father Sky. For when there is perfect alignment with source, anything is possible. There is nothing you cannot do. There is nothing you cannot be. Go, my child, explore!

I recalled my unexpected adventure into the realm of fairies as I stepped into their dimensional space on that morning walk in November 2018. It had awakened the child within, and a sense of wonderment filled my being.

Was I ready to take the angels' advice to explore our marvelous world? Yes, but it would not be through my eyes. It would be through the eyes of a child, one that walks hand in hand with the other-worldly beings of the fairies.

I want to live my life through the innocence of youth, knowing the Earth angels surround and protect me. I hear them calling, asking to play. Won't you join me?

CHAPTER 8: THE GIFT

The sound of *Jingle Bells* ringing from department stores was a persistent reminder the winter holidays were approaching. I had spent a good portion of the day window shopping, getting ideas for the grandchildren, Lorelai and Shalane. I would never have guessed the perfect gift would arrive that evening, but it wasn't for the girls, it was for me—a gift so monumental it would rock my world.

Retirement in June 2018 changed the landscape of my day-to-day living, and I could finally sleep past 5:00 a.m. By year's end, I had acclimated to my new schedule, substituting meditations for work meetings that had consumed me in the past. However, browsing department stores still felt like a luxury.

My watch told me it was time to switch gears and get ready for tonight's meditation. I had enough time to get home and prepare for my twice-monthly trip to Fort Myers. The drive usually takes an hour, but our population explodes during the winter months. As seasonal residents and visitors swarm to the warm, sandy shores of South Florida, the traffic pushes the thirty-mile commute to ninety minutes, sometimes more.

I arrived home, and twenty minutes later, I grabbed my journal, water, purse, and returned to the garage. After miles of slow and sometimes bumper-to-bumper traffic, I arrived at this interfaith, all faith church that had become my home away from home. I nestled into a lounge chair that I made more comfortable with a pillow and blankets from home. As is often the case, visions and messages began prior to the meditation. I opened my journal to document the production playing within my mind's eye.

Delicate sheets of pink threads drifted from above. Except for the color of the filaments, it looked like spun silk from an enormous floating spider's web. The church's dimmed lighting pierced the pastel gossamer strands, casting mesmerizing dancing shapes of light on the wall as endless layers sank into the room. I took a deep breath and descended into an exquisite wave of energy that washed over me.

The vibrations emanating from the web were unmistakable, and I knew we were in the presence of an angel. As layers of pink cobwebs enrobed the room, I intuitively knew its purpose was to bring peace and healing to all who would attend this meditation tonight. The message began:

December 17, 2018

I offer protection, divine protection to these most beloved ones. I give you the energy of peace, the energy of love, the energy of divine order.

As I journaled those words, the distant song of angels whispered in the background. Sheets of delicate pale fibers carpeted the floor, crystalizing into a thick, smooth pink layer.

I blinked my eyes in disbelief when tiny houses and buildings bubbled up from the glossy floor, creating a miniature village on the pink ice. It looked like a scene from Victorian London, straight from a Charles Dicken's novel. Gas-lit lampposts adorned tree-lined darkened streets. The reflection of candle-lit windows of multistoried houses glowed on snowy yards. Within moments, a crystal dome capped the miniature hamlet. My perspective zoomed back, and I realized the village was inside a snow globe small enough to fit in my palm.

I peered inside. Instinctively, I shook the globe, awakening it. I watched in amazement as flurries fell on the village's already snow-laden roofs and cobblestoned streets. The miniature version of nighttime Victorian London came alive. The gas-lit lampposts emitted a shimmering glow that danced in circles of golden light on the fallen snow. I was mesmerized by the meticulous details.

Time melted around me as I marveled at the beauty of this miniature winter wonderland nestled in my hand. I had an intuitive understanding of the dome covering the snow globe. I knew it safeguarded the village from outside disturbances. With this powerful protection in place, the snow continued to fall, and its hushed stillness brought a sense of serenity and peace to everything it touched. As I brought the sphere close to my heart and breathed in its tranquil energy, the message continued:

We are that protection. We install a globe of love around you and your precious world. We watch. We learn. Yes, we learn from you and your interactions, your thoughts, your emotions. We put forth energy that softens the pains and worries of those who need it.

Rest in peace, Dear Ones, for we are with you.

As I scribbled the last of these words in my journal, I noticed movement inside the globe. An ivory-colored object soared through the snow-filled sky. Its white body against the blinding snow rendered it almost invisible. Had it not been for its movement, I would not have seen it. I took a closer look; it was a snowy owl.

Reverend Bledsoe turned on the lights when the meditation ended, and I pulled out my jotted notes to report my experience. As I finished sharing, a smile spread across Reverend Bledsoe's face. She explained her reaction.

With everyone comfortably tucked into their spaces moments before the meditation began, Reverend Bledsoe did something she had never done before. She cast a protective dome of energy over the room. I smiled and nodded; she had just explained the genesis of the snow globe in my vision.

Without speaking, Reverend Bledsoe pointed to a Christmas tree against an interior wall. Because the overhead lights were off when I had entered the room, I had not seen it. My eyes scanned the tree from the bottom upward, branch by branch, absorbing the details of the decorations. When I reached the highest point, my mouth dropped open. Although I anticipated an angel or star would crown its top, I was wrong. Perched in this sacred place of honor was a snowy owl.

I took a deep breath and shook my head in disbelief as I marveled at the mystical snow-globe experience. A profound feeling of peace filled me. It was mid-December, and several holidays were approaching when many Jewish, Christian, and Buddhist people celebrate sacred events, filled with appreciation, compassion, love, and thoughtfulness. It is a time where goodwill and peace abound.

My thoughts returned to the distant voices of angels and the pink silky threads that had covered the room at the meditation's beginning. The energy accompanying the vision was unmistakably from angels, but there was something different.

Over the years of communication with the nonphysical, I had come to recognize pastel pink and green wisps as a telltale sign of angels. This vision had the soft energy of pink, but the green was missing. Why was it different? What did it mean?

The explanation flashed into my awareness in words that were not mine. I knew the answer. The blessed angelic energy that had ushered the vision of the village was from the Angel of Peace.

Pink has been one of my favorite colors for years, but I

wondered why it was the Angel of Peace's signature. I took a short detour and searched online for meaning. I had long known the delicate color of pink is associated with tenderness and universal love, but I wanted more information.

Color-meaning's website reveals pink "inspires us to cling to hope."[14] There are no obstacles too significant that pink cannot overcome. "Leading with passion, kindness, and understanding, the color pink embodies all that is good in the world. Pink seeks to make others feel accepted by offering an unmatched level of sympathy."

Another website, Graf1x.com, reports pink is associated with love, tranquility, and nurturing "while conveying a sense of safety."[15] The color's sensitivity is from the passion of red combined with the purity of white. It represents the sweetness and innocence of the child.

I smiled when I learned of pink's protective qualities; the symbolism of the glass dome covering the snowy hamlet now makes sense. This brief research on this perfect color made me appreciate its connection to the Angel of Peace. It's a match made in heaven, and it's logical this divine being surrounds us during sacred holidays, but what about the snowy owl? Why was this magnificent bird connected to the Angel of Peace?

My awareness returned to the room at Church of Spiritual Light. My ears perked when I heard Reverend Bledsoe say her master totem was a snowy owl. I was not familiar with the term "master totem," but I knew I would research it later.

I took a deep breath as I marveled at my magical snow-globe vision. Others shared their experiences, and I could only smile as person after person described seeing angels and other winged beings. Someone felt an angel's wing brush against them. Many

---

14 https://www.color-meanings.com/pink-color-meaning-the-color-pink/

15 https://graf1x.com/color-psychology-emotion-meaning-poster/

reported feelings of serenity, peace, and calm.

There were undeniable similarities, and this impressed me because we perceive experiences through personal filters. This group validation spoke to the greater truth that we were in the presence of the Angel of Peace.

A few days later, Reverend Bledsoe emailed me information about the spiritual interpretation of her master totem, and a deeper understanding of the experience emerged. I learned the snowy owl is a messenger that delivers omens and information from the nonphysical to the physical, but more than that, he is a protector. Had Reverend Bledsoe's master totem guided her to build the bubble of protection around the room?

I searched for more meaning. The Legends of America website reported totems are spirit beings, sacred objects, or symbols of a tribe, clan, family, or individual.[16] Although different animal spirit guides or power animals may come and go depending on circumstances, a master totem remains for life. It is the primary guardian spirit that protects in the physical and nonphysical dimensions.

According to Reverend Bledsoe's Addiction Alchemy website, the snowy owl signifies purity of light that helps us work in the darkness to bring back deeply tucked-away secrets.[17] The snowy owl is connected with the mysteries of the universe because it sees beyond the illusions of time. It represents the soul's ascension to higher levels of thought and consciousness.

The website reveals the snowy owl follows those with the gift of channeling to help discern the teachings correctly. Is this what had happened to me? Without a doubt, I knew the Angel of Peace had ushered the experience with the snowy owl inside the magical snow globe.

---

16 www.legendsofamerica.com/na-totems/

17 www.addictionalchemy.com/snowyowl/

The presence of a snowy owl represents a new level of spiritual maturity and wisdom, one that stems from "still and calm observation." That last sentence from Addiction Alchemy's website brought cold chills that wrapped my body from head to feet, a sign for me that represented a validation of truths. I knew to pay attention.

Still and calm observation? That described my life. I had observed, documented, and eventually embraced the channeled messages and visions that had begun in August 2013. By accepting them, I had grown to a level of spiritual maturity well beyond my pre-awakened state, precisely what the website suggested when a snowy owl makes his presence known.

The snow-globe adventure, including the messages from the Angel of Peace and the experience with the snowy owl, was very powerful. It was, indeed, a gift, one I would treasure for years to come. I knew my future winter holiday seasons would never be the same, knowing the Angel of Peace protects and surrounds us with the energy of love.

I would have been satisfied had the experience stopped there, but the second installment of my holiday gift was about to be delivered. Four days later, I woke early and smiled. It was my birthday, and I couldn't think of a better way to celebrate than to attend Friday's morning meditation at Goddess I Am. After a leisurely breakfast of Cheerios and coffee, I grabbed my light jacket and journal and headed to my car for the short drive.

I arrived early and parked my car. The weather was too cool to wait outside for the doors to open, so I unbuckled my seatbelt to relax while I enjoyed the warmth from my car's heated seat. Within seconds, an inner vision began, so I grabbed my phone to record the details.

Soft pink clouds of energy surrounded me. I breathed in divine serenity, and I immediately knew the Angel of Peace had arrived. I found myself rising upward, outside of my car. I soared over Goddess I Am, watching its green tin roof shrink from view as I sailed higher into the atmosphere.

Far above the Earth, I stopped. I looked around and saw nothing but soft pink waves. It was a feeling of comfort and protection. The rolling tide moved toward me and swaddled me like a newborn. While floating in this perfect space, the following message arrived:

December 21, 2018

A birth, a rebirth, a renewal. The moon is at her fullest, like a mother ready to birth her child. We look upon those in the Earth plane with love and compassion. We seek those whose hearts have opened—those hearts, like a full moon, that are ready to spill forth the words of love and compassion.

The Angel of Peace and her minions surround you, softening the edges of worry, breaking those bonds that encompass you and blind you to the truth that we are all one.

Today is a day of unity, a day of fullness, and birth. Be ye rebirthed and awaken to the power that lies within. Know that we are like that guiding light that brought forth the wise men to the birth of the one most holy.

Let go of your resentments. Let go of those things that bind you and to that which does not serve you.

Be ye one with spirit. Take a deep breath and allow this breath of life to enter your field of awareness, for this is the time that our energies are called forth to assist. Know that we are here, supporting you, watching over you with love. We are upholding you as you step into your empowerment.

You are a beacon; you are light. Be a guiding light to others. Allow your guiding light to shine as you walk your path of truth. Know that your heart guides you as well as others.

As your light grows, so will your vision. Some only see a

*few steps ahead on their path of truth, but with increased light
comes increased sight. Lift your heart so that you may see. Lift
your eyes so that your way will be lighted. Start walking the
path of truth, the path of love, the path of light, and all will be
well.*

In my mind's eye, I saw myself walking. Unlike the usual
bird's-eye view in my visions, I could only see mid-calf downward
as I traveled in what appeared to be a meadow. Although the sun
warmed my back, it must have been early; morning dew still clung
to the grasses beneath the soles of my bare feet.

As I moved, a vibration in my heart compelled me to fill my
lungs with the fresh air that surrounded me. With each great
exhalation, my perspective changed, and I realized each breath
propelled me upward until I had reached an aerial view.

The vision represented a literal translation of the messenger's
words of lifting my heart so I might see. I also understood the
reasoning why my initial view was so restricted. The mid-calf
downward perspective made me realize all of life's journeys begin
with taking that first step.

My limited viewpoint, however, had not deterred me. With
each purposeful stride, I embodied confidence, building more
trust in the process. It was the trust, the faith that had set the
foundation for the higher perspective that had catapulted me to
the above-the-ground view in the vision.

With that realization came another dramatic shift. In an instant,
I rocketed to a point at least a mile above my current position. As I
looked below where the other-me walked, I noticed many others.
Their treks paralleled mine across the grasslands that expanded
beyond what my eyes could see.

Like me at the beginning of this process, they seemed unaware
of the others. They did not understand their solo treks were part
of a collective, significant movement but toward what? Were they

approaching enlightenment? Perhaps so.

As I thought about the message and the vision, I realized the more important life lesson: When we connect to angels and other similar energies, we begin to recognize the subtle cues that guide us. Trust and faith become fodder to ignite these connections and allow more wisdom to enter.

We are not alone; there are no solo treks. We are part of a more significant movement across this expansive universe. Learning to access the gentle guidance from angels brings a level of comfort in knowing we are part of a grander scheme.

There were many vital elements to consider from this experience. This message, calling for us to embrace birth, rebirth, and renewal, arrived on a day that is special for me—my birthday. Only four days later, millions of Christians in the United States would celebrate another birth. For over two thousand years, families have gathered around the world to commemorate the birth of the Christ child.

The date of this message also has astrological importance, marking a transitional period as days become longer in the Northern Hemisphere and shorter in the Southern Hemisphere. This winter solstice was adorned by a full moon, something that won't occur again on December 21 until 2094, according to Forbes website.[18]

The Ursid meteor shower rained down in the Northern Hemisphere just after midnight, adding a perfect touch to this already special night. The shooting stars were the proverbial icing on the cake, making my birthday a fantastic night, indeed.

The message from the Angel of Peace pleads with us to seek others with hearts filled with love and compassion. So often we speak to what divides us, not what unites us. This divine guidance

---

18 https://www.forbes.com/sites/trevornace/2018/12/18/winter-solstice-2018-coincides-with-both-a-full-moon-and-meteor-shower/#23011f2452e6

requests we open ourselves to the truth of unity.

Knowing the Angel of Peace watches over us gives me great peace and solace, but this was also a message of empowerment as she guides humanity to step into the path of truth. By embracing rebirth, perhaps we will begin to feel the spirit of unity.

I spent the last day of 2018 at home while thousands gathered near Naples Pier to celebrate the year's end by watching fireworks. The pier is only four miles away, but why give up my front-row seat from my backyard?

I gathered a blanket and my phone to use as a flashlight and headed to the beach. I strolled a couple hundred feet until I found an ideal place to view the light show. I was close enough to see bursts of color in the sky yet far enough away to soften the loud, startling booms that send dogs under their owners' beds.

The spot was perfect. If I turned around, I could see smaller cascades of colorful light from the fireworks at Fort Myers Beach and Sanibel Island that lit the dark skies to my north. After the event ended, I sat on the beach to catch the stream of lights from the Gulf of Mexico as more than fifty boats raced home from their waterfront view of the fireworks.

As the lights whizzed past me, I thought of these past two weeks of 2018. I had felt the Angel of Peace as she smoothed the sometimes-hectic energies woven into this festive season. It was such a blessing to have her with me.

After ten or fifteen minutes, I gathered my belongings and walked the short distance home. This holiday season was almost over, and I was ready to welcome 2019 with open arms. I would sleep in tomorrow and wake, eager to see what this new year might bring.

I began 2019 by attending an event at Goddess I Am. The meditation focused on the spirit of the holiday season, and it allowed the participants to reflect on the past few weeks of 2018.

As I listened to background music, I found myself drifting

away from my physical body. My breath seemed to propel me upward, and with each inhalation, my speed increased. Within seconds I zoomed through the ethers like snow in a blizzard. Hundreds of other sparkling structures blurred past me including snowflakes, stars, and crystalline orbs.

Without warning, I came to a full halt, and I found myself floating in a peaceful sea of tranquility. I opened my eyes and realized my energy body had transformed; I had become a multifaceted crystal. Hundreds of thousands of twinkling bright lights surrounded me, flashing against the dark void of deep space. I realized I could see everything around me without moving; I had a 360-degree field of vision.

Time stood still as I floated in this perfect space. Had an hour passed or just a few seconds? Something interrupted my hypnotic state, that feeling you get when you realize you are not alone. Who or what was this? I felt fluttering within my chest and realized this presence had come from my heart.

I took a deep breath and held it for several seconds. As I exhaled, a puff of pink clouds billowed around me. My heart reached up in silent recognition that I was in the company of a divine being—the Angel of Peace had returned.

In slow-motion, she wrapped her wings around me, encompassing me in a blanket of bliss, love, and tenderness. I felt like a baby in its mother's arms—warm, protected, and adored beyond measure.

With the glow from the Angel of Peace surrounding me, I realized I was in the space of things that could not be defined. I looked at my crystalline body, and I intuitively knew it represented fragments of the divine spark of source. It was alive, vibrant, and unique to me.

I understood the stillness and silence of the meditation had allowed me to enter into a higher state of being. I was in a space of expanded awareness, and it was this burgeoning of consciousness that had made the angel connection possible. The message began:

January 4, 2019

We are always around, Dear One, but not every soul can perceive our energies. Let go of notions. Let go of your concepts of angels. Some see us with wings; others do not. It is not the physical form that is important, but it is the consciousness of love that reaches out between the dimensions to make contact possible.

Know that we are here and always have been. We are your guiding light. We are that whisper that directs you to a different path. Know that we live within your heart. Rejoice with us, for this time of year is the time for love to be shared upon your most blessed planet.

The time for change is nigh. We shall guide you into the path of peace.

The vision of me surrounded by other crystalline entities replayed in my mind's eye. My energy body had transformed into a crystal structure, but I was still me. Although my external features changed, I hadn't. It must be the same for angels. With or without wings, with or without a physical form, it didn't matter; their consciousness of love still existed.

The meditation ended and I gathered my belongings to leave. Driving home, questions flew through my mind about the past three meditations. I entered my apartment and dropped into a chair in the living room. Deep in thought, I stared out the window.

I recalled my adventures into the mystical realm of angels. There are so many mysteries in this world, and we cannot begin to understand even half of them. We wander in the dark, seeking truth among the shadows. But every once in a while, a glimmer of hope shines, lighting a path of wisdom for all to see.

That flicker in the dark had come from the Angel of Peace

as she blessed us with gifts of guidance, love, and peace. As that thought entered my mind, I looked up to see a blaze of sunlight as it pierced the cloudy sky. A shaft of light, much more brilliant than sunshine, flooded the room. It engulfed me as I sat in my chair, bathing me with more than mere warmth. This was the energy of tenderness and affection. I smiled as I realized this was from the Angel of Peace.

Nestled deep in my chair, I soaked in this divine light and took a deep breath. Tears of joy slid down my face as I realized meeting the Angel of Peace was a gift, a perfect gift, a gift I would cherish for years to come.

CHAPTER 9
METATRON PART 1: THE FOUNDATION

I felt myself slip through a rip in the fabric of the universe. Darkness engulfed me as I struggled to cling to consciousness. As the room whirled around me, I succumbed and tumbled further into the abyss. I was not dreaming; this scenario happened in my hometown of Naples, Florida, as I stepped across a threshold that would forever change me.

Summer 2016 was approaching, and I was eager to plan my time off work. After receiving messages from the nonphysical for almost three years, I was ready for more exploration. Since August 2013, my frame of reference had expanded until these experiences had become my new normal. I had grown accustomed to the unusual and comfortable with the uncomfortable, but I hungered for more.

I searched for information, seeking new paths to quench my ever-increasing thirst for more spiritual experiences. When I heard Sandra McGill would be hosting a series of Archangel Metatron meditations, I jumped at this opportunity for a new adventure. Metatron. Although I had heard the name before, I did not know of him.

It was the end of May. As I ticked the days off my calendar until the end of the school year, I hoped this new class would help jump-start my summer break. I entered Sandra's address in my phone and engaged the GPS. It was less than nine miles away, a twenty-two-minute drive.

I pulled into her condominium's parking lot early and waited. Ten minutes later, a few cars arrived at the same time, and when the occupants walked toward Sandra's door, I followed.

My innate shyness reared its ugly head, so I paid my fee and searched for the quietest corner of the room. As people entered Sandra's home, it was apparent they knew each other well. They were lively, sometimes shouting friends' names as they crossed the front door's threshold. People hugged and soon the room filled with laughter and conversations that became louder by the minute. A couple of women looked familiar, and they acknowledged my presence by a smile or a nod.

I was a newcomer and felt like the new kid in town—out of place. I was surprised by the large number in attendance. There were very few people in Naples in my spiritual orbit, yet a tight-knit clique was right here in Sandra's living room. Although I felt like a fifth wheel, deep within the recesses of my heart, I wondered whether I had found my tribe.

It was a full house. People took their seats, and silence fell over the room as Sandra connected with those who were attending via the Internet. It was time for the class to begin. Sandra started with introductions then explained the structure for the meetings.

The class would begin by each inhouse participant choosing an oracle card and Sandra drawing cards for those attending online. Next, Lee Shook would conduct an angel wash, followed by the energy downloads from Metatron that Sandra would lead. The final activity of each class would be a discussion of the oracle cards.

I had taken several Seraphim Blueprint classes by this time, so I was familiar with energy activations. I had also experienced an angel wash at an event at a local church a few weeks before, but I was curious. I wanted more information on these powerful washes.

As I was writing this book, I interviewed Lee and Sandra to understand the genesis of the angel wash. While chatting over a casual meal at First Watch, I discovered Sandra and Lee had channeled this process. The procedure only takes five or six minutes, but its effects are long-lasting.

Although initially designed as an integral part of the Angel Codes of Peace initiative, the value of the angel wash was readily recognized, and its implementation became widespread. The wash is similar to clearing and preparing a canvas before an artist begins a work of inspiration.

Sandra and Lee compare the angel wash to an automatic car wash, complete with stations to clean and balance the body's energy centers. Each person enters what I refer to as a cosmic automatic conveyor belt. From that point, Archangel Metatron and Saint Anthony process the energies.

It is not easy to understand events and activities from the nonphysical, and to describe them is often tricky. Because we filter our experiences through our energy fields and our cultural conditioning, a shared nonphysical event sometimes manifests differently. But this was not the case with the angel wash; the analogy was as powerful as it was appropriate.

An automatic car wash is simple. The driver turns off the engine, puts the car in neutral, and the machine does the rest. An electric eye measures the car to adjust the stations for those specific dimensions. A conveyor belt pulls the vehicle through a tunnel with hanging curtains of long fabric strips that swish back and forth to sponge in deep-cleaning foam. Cylindrical scrubbers with hundreds of small cloth strips spin along the car's vertical surfaces, followed by rotating high-pressure jets that rinse the loosened dirt. The vehicle is now clean.

The car exits through a dryer arch that forces massive amounts of hot air through multiple nozzles. By the time the vehicle disengages from the conveyor belt, it has been measured, foamed, scrubbed, rinsed, and dried. It exits like new, shining from wheels to roof.

The angel wash isn't that much different. Intelligent angelic frequencies adjust the levels of cleaning and balancing according to each person's specific need and energy field. We disengage our engines and set our gears in neutral by closing our eyes and taking a few relaxing breaths. Once we are in this meditative state of acceptance, we open to the frequencies of the wash. The angels do the rest, and we exit the cosmic conveyor belt anew.

As Lee began the angel wash, we settled into our chairs, but as I closed my eyes, something pierced the darkness. A rhombus had formed a few inches in front of me. It looked like the diamond in a deck of playing cards, but it wasn't red, it was made from crystal. It pulsed like a heart, and with each beat, its iridescent sides threw dancing spots of rainbow-colored lights into the ethers.

The diamond slipped into my forehead and stopped briefly before sinking through the middle of my spine. When the crystal rhombus reached the center of my body, it stopped again and began to stretch until it had extended several feet beyond my physical form.

While in its expanded state, a radiant line inched along an invisible arc between the diamond's four points. It reminded me of the trail of light that follows the glowing tips of sparklers on Independence Day. Soon the curved trajectory of the radiance encased the entire rhombus within its circle of light.

A horizontal beam shot from the widest points of the diamond, separating it into two pieces. In response, Metatron spoke the following:

May 31, 2016

Similar to the equator that surrounds Earth, this point represents a division. It is a division between as above and so below. This divine point is a space where magic occurs.

The me in the vision began to move. My arms and legs stretched until they reached the outer perimeter of the light sphere. I was surprised to see I had two sets of arms and legs. The palms of my two lower hands faced down while my other palms faced up.

The four-armed-four-legged me remained still as the flat, two-dimensional diamond stretched and morphed into a square. The circle and a square surrounded my body; I realized I had become a twin image of Leonardo da Vinci's Vitruvian Man.[19]

While suspended in this da Vinci look-alike, I felt sensations in my downward-facing palms, as if they were magnetized. Tight waves of energy entered the soles of my feet and exploded upward in a fan of brilliant light particles that abruptly ended at my outstretched arms. This spray of energy created an inverted triangle, mirroring the lower half of the original diamond that had entered my forehead.

A similar tingling in my two upward-facing palms drew energy from above. Light poured through the top of my head and morphed into a downward cascading shower of photons that stopped at my arms. This triangle of light covered my upper body, looking very much like the top half of the crystal rhombus.

The energy surges from above and below had empowered the mirror-twin triangles covering me, and they began to transform. Within seconds, they morphed into three-dimensional triangular pyramids, also known as tetrahedrons.

I initially thought the two tetrahedrons touched, but closer

---

19 https://leonardodavinci.stanford.edu/submissions/clabaugh/history/leonardo.html

inspection revealed a small space between them. This gap held the laser-thin beam I had seen earlier. It was the equator, the *division between as above and so below* that Metatron had referenced.

On some undefined level, I understood the me in the vision was an active part of this transformation, but how? Had I called these energies? I didn't know, but I knew that somehow, this two-pyramidal form had empowered me.

Thunderous vibrations from deep within Earth's core rippled through the air, and the equator wavered in response. It felt like a precursor to a cataclysmic event like a volcanic eruption or an earthquake, but I soon realized it wasn't. It was the awakening of an ancient device or machine.

Sounding like a boulder creaking open from a medieval tomb, the two tetrahedrons moved closer, swallowing the laser-thin beam that had divided them. There was no longer separation between top and bottom. They continued moving together until they were completely merged; the double pyramids had become one, producing a star tetrahedron.

As the shape formed, my awareness dropped into a peaceful sea of tranquility. Something very surprising was going on in my mind, and I realized the true me lived deep within this form. Outer conditions had no power over me. As this epiphany washed through my awareness, I remained calm, drifting further into a mysterious ocean of serenity and unspeakable beauty.

Sandra called us back into the room. I grabbed a tissue from my purse and dabbed my tear-streaked face. During the short angel wash, I had traveled outside the constraints of time as I knew it, swimming in ancient, wordless knowledge beyond my human understanding. I had tasted the divine and hungered for more.

We finished the other exercises for the evening and said our goodbyes. As I gathered my belongings to head out the door, I couldn't help but compare this class to others I had attended. It was so different. Although Metatron had communicated only three sentences, my experiences were intense and far-reaching. For whatever reason, I understood wisdom would come through these events and not just the spoken word.

I was hungry for more information, but I've always feared an early search might taint future events. Even if it didn't, doubt would enter, convincing me it had. So, I'd wait until the classes ended before conducting any online research. Until then, I'd have to be contented to wonder what these experiences meant. I don't know why or how I had been granted this mystical, adventurous journey, but it was more than I had hoped for. I was curious to see what the next class might bring.

A week later, I started my car and smiled as I drove the nine miles to Sandra's home. I was eager to attend this second class, but I was more excited that there was just one more workday before the summer break. Then, only two more years until retirement. Although I was tired from the strain and drain that accompanies ending another school year, I was thrilled about the upcoming time off. Yes, I could see the light at the end of the tunnel.

I pulled into the parking lot, gathered my belongings, and stepped inside Sandra's home. Once everyone online and inhouse had gathered, we drew cards from another oracle deck and settled comfortably in our seats for the initiations. A vision had begun, and I rushed to document it before class started.

A time-lapsed rerun from last week played in my mind's eye. The upright and inverted triangular pyramids began to merge in slow motion to form the star tetrahedron, and I, like da Vinci's Vitruvian Man's doppelganger, was suspended in the center.

The overlapping tetrahedrons stalled, and I noticed a vital organ floated in the center of each: my heart in the upper and my uterus in the lower. An almost imperceptible nudge guided me to look more closely at the image. A smile painted my face when I realized the similar shapes of both organs; the two pyramids had hearts.

The heart centers of both tetrahedrons converged like magnets, and I heard the words "zero point." I had no idea what that meant, but I had long ago understood more information would be forthcoming, and if I didn't learn about it from the messengers, I'd research it after the classes ended.

I finished scribbling my experience in my journal and looked around. Everyone was sitting with eyes closed; Lee had begun her angel wash. A swirl of hot energy circled my ears. This burning was a new sensation for me, and I wondered what it represented.

Last week's rhombus-shaped crystal reappeared in front of my eyes, and like the previous class, it entered my forehead and implanted itself in my skull. The center of the diamond began to glow like a hot ember. Was this the heat that had caused my ears to burn?

A laser beam burst from this fiery diamond and shot down the center of my spine. It stopped where the two hearts of the tetrahedrons had connected, the center of the pyramids. A message from Metatron began:

June 7, 2016

This is the zero point.

As these words entered my awareness, the beam from the star tetrahedron's hearts separated into two streams of light that traveled along my outstretched da Vinci arms. The lights looped around the fingertips of my hands, then reverted back to a single shaft of light when it returned to my spinal cord.

The light continued its downward path, blasting through my feet and deep into the ground. Simultaneously, a second shaft of light exploded from the top of the diamond embedded in my head and zoomed upward into the sky.

My vision panned to a bird's-eye view, and I realized a cross of light was embedded in my body, connecting above to below and spanning side-to-side. I was a living, breathing, pulsating crucifix of energy. The message continued:

The cross is the foundation of the merkaba, connecting above to below, encompassing everything around it. It is the birthing of a new energy body. The center where the two hearts meet is the zero point which can travel upon the timeline of life.

Another name had just emerged for the star tetrahedron: merkaba. I had not heard this term before, but I would put it on my list to research later. The message continued:

This one can step into the timeless nature of existence and move in the direction that beckons. Move to the past and heal all karmic debt so that it will not interfere with generations to come. Move to the future to heal that which might appear.

It is a birthing. This foundation born upon you is a new body, a body of light. It is charged by vibrations of the utmost high. There is nothing it cannot do. There is nothing you cannot do, for you are empowered with divine light.

I bestow upon you the light of the ages, the light that led the wise men to the Christ child. This is the light of the divine, the light of wisdom, the light of truth. It is the lighted path of the Buddha, our most beloved Enlightened One. It is the lighted path upon which all ascended masters have trod.

We give you this roadmap. It is yours. It is within you and always has been. We have only lit the path for you to see. You must take the first step upon this path of wisdom. We are with you, and we shall remain by your side as you traverse this path for which you are destined.

The class ended, and it was time to say my goodbyes and head home. I stumbled in a fog of confusion as I tried to embrace and understand the evening's events. There was so much to unwrap, not only from the messages but from this and the first class. It seemed my experiences brought more questions than answers, and I hoped with time, clarity would arrive.

Until then, I knew these forms, from the living crucifix of light to the diamonds, triangles, and tetrahedrons, had somehow empowered me. I was beginning to see the importance of my interactions with them. Although I didn't understand their purpose, I felt a sense of peace and serenity that the shapes had brought into my life.

It was the middle of June, and I was ready for the third class. I had basked in my summer vacation for almost a week, feeling that welcomed sense of renewal that comes with a break from work. I was eager to see what this next session might offer, so I gathered my things and headed to my car.

The drive to Sandra's was uneventful. Naples returns to its sleepy-town status in the summer, so there was little traffic on the roads. I parked, gathered my belongings, entered her apartment, and sought a spot to settle. I put my purse and other things in a back row of folding chairs adjacent to the dining area. Scooting my seat back a few feet would put me at the dining table. Writing in my journal would be much more comfortable. I grinned as I realized I had found my perfect spot.

With money in my hand, I walked to the center of the room to pay. As I returned to settle in my area, several people nodded, and a couple of participants hugged me. I was feeling more comfortable and less like an outsider. I was excited to begin.

As Sandra connected with the online group, we drew from Doreen Virtue's Archangel Oracle Cards. I slipped my card into the back of my journal without looking at it. A vision had begun, and I scrambled to document these events unfolding in my mind's eye.

A diamond-shaped figure floated near the top of the ceiling. Although it looked identical to the rhombus that had entered my forehead during the first two classes, I knew it wasn't. Although my eyes could not distinguish the difference, I intuitively knew this was a star.

It became three dimensional and began to spin. Its slow-motion revolutions sprinkled an iridescent trail of light as if from a magic wand. I knew this was extraordinary and powerful energy.

Within seconds, the spinning structure covered the room in a two-foot-high hill of stardust. I watched in amazement as the center of the mound collapsed, creating a funnel in the middle of Sandra's living room. The light particles swirled and tumbled down this cosmic drain.

The observer-me followed the cascading stardust several feet below the floor where it began to take form. An identical three-dimensional star materialized from the swirling particles; the star from above had birthed another.

The gravitational pull stretched between the two luminous figures like a suspension bridge, connecting the star above with the one below. I don't know how I knew this, but I understood this link was sacred, and it represented perfect balance.

Without warning, I became breathless and shaken. I felt myself start to spin as darkness engulfed me. I struggled to maintain my equilibrium and hold onto my consciousness, but I could not. I succumbed to the whirling room and felt myself tumble into a dark abyss that was as inky and deep as a black hole, but why was the blackness so dazzling? While swimming in this magnificent, mighty ocean of energy, time stood still, and then I heard the words of Metatron:

June 14, 2016

Step into this most divine energy. This is needed for expanding consciousness; it is a prerequisite for healing. This energy is universal as it connects to the divine above and the sacred below.

The spinning stopped as quickly as it had begun. The gravitational bridge dissolved, pulling the two stars together until they merged. I was mesmerized by its dazzling beauty. Reflected light from its multifaceted sides sequined the room in miniature prisms of splendor.

Similar to the previous classes, the two halves of the stunning three-dimensional star divided into two triangular pyramids before merging into a star tetrahedron. By now, I'd come to understand this shape as a prerequisite for Metatron; it was his cue to enter.

Now that the stage was set, it was time for the angel wash. I closed my eyes and took a few deep breaths as Lee began. I had no idea that things were about to get very interesting.

Within seconds, the star tetrahedron began to spin, spewing a trail of tiny stars from its center. It mirrored the actions of the ceiling star I'd seen at the beginning of class except for one bizarre difference—this one was inside my skull.

It radiated intense heat. Its centrifugal force pushed the light stream through my scalp in an endless wave of tiny star-shaped photons that whirled over the top of my head like a dazzling crown of light. I heard the following:

This is a crown of energy, much like what was worn by the Christ child and other ascended masters.

In my mind's eye, multiple saints with brilliant halos above their heads flashed before me, and I understood these circles of light were the energy crowns Metatron referenced. Although I hesitate to identify mine as a halo, I knew it had originated from the zero point or ground-state energy inside my skull.

160

I had heard the words "zero point" when the centers of the pyramidal triangles had merged to form a star tetrahedron during the first class. A crucifix of light had formed in the second class, with its center also superimposed over my heart space. I began to understand why Metatron said the zero point was the *foundation of the merkaba* and the basis for a new body of light. It was the heart that was the key for transformation to occur.

As mention of zero point threaded its way into class three, I gained a better understanding. An unexpected thought pierced my awareness. I knew zero-point energy had manifested as a crown of light, but I intuitively knew I could use it as a tool to activate other energy centers in my body.

The crown began to sink through my skull. An intense wave of vibrations moved from the top of my scalp to my eyebrows. When the crown reached my orbital sockets, it collapsed into its former zero-point state, and just as quickly, morphed into a jagged, spinning disk. Sparks spewed as the flattened crown's whirling blade sliced through my skull as efficiently as an electric circular saw.

My heart hammered in my chest as the top of my head lifted, creating a five-inch gap. A whisper slipped into my awareness, telling me my vision was clearing. The message continued:

It is the opening of the divine. It is the space between words, the space between thought, for that is where I will reside. Come with me. Come with me on this path of wisdom and clarity.

The gentle words of Metatron seemed to soften the explicit and graphic details spinning in my mind's eye. I had no time to process this extraordinary experience because the next activation began immediately. I gave a deep sigh of relief when I realized I was exiting this much too-detailed scene.

A fierce surge of heat permeated my body, and the intensity

indicated there would be no relief in sight. The last experience had not ended; there was more to come. As my feverish body shivered, the newly created space at my forehead began to expand. Metatron spoke:

Step into this perfect space. Allow yourself to enter. This allowing will send you where you need to go. Its guidance is divine.

I saw myself floating on a beam of light, and I wondered whether my experience was similar to the famous light-beam rider, Albert Einstein. Was this the path of wisdom and clarity alluded to by Metatron? Would it send me where I needed to go?

We took a break when the second activation ended. I spent a few minutes reviewing my notes to make sure I could read my writing. It seems the longer I wait, the more my words resemble hieroglyphics.

After reviewing my notes, I took a drink of water and stood to stretch. It was time for a restroom break. When I placed my journal on my chair, something fell and glided to the floor. It was the oracle card I had tucked inside my notebook at the beginning of class. My mouth dropped open as I picked it up and saw its title: Clairvoyance. The subtitle indicated the angels were helping my spiritual sight to awaken so I could fully see heavenly love.

The card was accurate; an angel had, indeed, assisted me. Through Archangel Metatron, the whirling cosmic blade inside my skull had created a literal clearing for my spiritual eyesight. In case I hadn't understood my experiences, the oracle card served as a backup. My eyes crinkled into a smile at the synchronicity, all the while wishing Metatron had used a different example, one with less explicit details.

The break ended, and we moved seamlessly to the next exercise. I quickly learned another chapter of my clairvoyance activity was about to begin. Apparently, opening my spiritual eyes would require more action.

A different sensation settled across my eyebrows, yet I knew it was from the same spinning blade that had open my skull. Gentle waves of peace, love, and compassion trickled down my head to the center of my chest.

Insight flooded my awareness as if a fog had lifted. I knew the heart space was in the center of the star tetrahedron where Metatron resides, but I began to understand the magic of the zero point. I intuitively knew this location was a portal to the divine.

With this new realization, things started to happen. Layers of fine mist shrouded the area between my physical heart and the double heart of the star tetrahedron. This heart space remained motionless while the two pyramidal halves began to spin in opposite directions: the top half counterclockwise, the lower half clockwise.

My awareness slipped inside the rotating machine, and I accelerated through the cosmos as if I had entered a wormhole in deep space. I blasted out the other side and into an infinite fog of peace and tranquility. Light surrounded me.

I tried to get my bearings as I experienced the world through this dazzling prism of consciousness, but I could no longer tell where my body ended and the surroundings began. I was still me, but I had dissolved into the infinite universe. While in this state of complete surrender and ultimate knowing, I heard the following:

There is an understanding that has not been present before, for you have tapped into the River of Consciousness, the River of Light, the river that contains all there is.

Questions exploded inside my brain like fireworks, but words got lost on the way to my mouth. There was no vocabulary to describe what I felt. Metatron's star tetrahedron had transported me beyond space and time and allowed me to dip my toes into the eternal waters of all that is. The sweet taste of infinity, like a giant luminous star, sparked hope for humanity across our planet and beyond.

A memory flashed into my mind. The star tetrahedron reminded me of the machine in the 1997 movie *Contact* that transported Dr. Ellie Arroway, played by Jodi Foster, into another dimension. She, too, had stepped out of time, yet those observing her did not share her perspective.

I sank further in my chair, wondering what had happened. My experiences were profound, and yet I dared not share them. Without having a frame of reference for what had occurred, I couldn't begin to explain it to others.

The room fell silent as we prepared for the evening's last event. Night had fallen, and moonlight glittered across the floor from the lanai's windows. A velvety comfort swept through me, and I intuitively knew I was shifting and adapting to the experiences with these shapes.

With fondness, I thought about the initial class. The Metatron energies had begun with a diamond-shaped rhombus that had entered my forehead. As that image came to mind, the following message arrived:

Call upon this diamond at will, for it is a tool for you to use. It is the heart of the merkaba. It is the purity and the power of the light of the divine.

This diamond represented the keystone for Metatron's sweeping energies. This shape had ushered in Metatron with each class, and now it represented the foundation for my changing energy field. I felt a sense of empowerment when I realized it served as a tool I could use when needed.

An understanding washed over me, and I began to comprehend

the experiential nature of my encounters with Archangel Metatron. Insights would no longer arrive neatly woven in the often-poetic conversations with the nonphysical. Instead, they would be through my interactions with forms and shapes.

The importance of these past three classes had become apparent. Metatron had installed a framework, a system of forms, that little by little, adapted to me and found a niche in my energy field. It had been a steady process, but the die had been cast, and there was no turning back.

I was in new territory, but these classes whetted my appetite for more. I stood at the door with no expectations, but with excitement and curiosity, ready for anything the next class might offer.

CHAPTER 10
METATRON PART 2: DISCOVERING TRUTH

Truth is fluid, changing its course over time like a river. Throughout the years, I learned what I chose to believe had little to do with fact. This statement was never more apparent than in the period immediately following the Metatron classes.

As I gathered evidence supporting my experiences, it rocked the foundation of my beliefs. I discovered truths that were outside my knowledge, firmly placing these episodes in the outer fringes of the bell curve of normalcy. Yet deep within me, something else stirred, and a sudden understanding much larger than words surfaced. I knew I had come face-to-face with universal truths that would change my views of life.

I had progressed with each class, and the Metatron interactions felt profound. I knew I was evolving, yet my logical resistance would kick in when things seemed too strange. When faced with these novel and sometimes bizarre experiences, I silently objected, and I would revert to my professional training as a psychologist and demand data.

Seeking new information wasn't anything new for me; many

questions had surfaced since my spontaneous opening to the nonphysical in August 2013. Over time, I had learned to trust my explorations into the unknown, so I delved deeper into the unmarked territories of spirit.

A two-week break left me feeling refreshed and eager to resume. After stacking my dinner plate in the dishwasher, I looked out the large window in my living room and marveled at the beauty of the late afternoon sun as it hung low in the sky. It would be another beautiful sunset, but I would miss it. It was time to head to Sandra's home.

Excitement flooded through me while en route to the meeting; I could hardly wait for the class to begin. I parked my car, entered Sandra's apartment, and headed toward my favorite spot at the dining table. I chatted with a few people and realized what a difference a few months had made. I had begun this course as a stranger, but today I felt I was among friends.

After introductory activities and connecting with the online participants, the class was ready to begin. As the angel wash started, something odd happened. Although I didn't know it at the time, I was about to experience Metatron and St. Anthony as they adjusted the frequencies of the angel wash to my specific energy field.

A series of sensations simultaneously permeated my body. A dull ache on the left side of the back of my skull seemed to compete with the tapping behind my right knee. Ripples of vibrations swirled around my heart as tingles flooded down my arms and out both hands. After about ten seconds, these separate vibrations abruptly stopped then coalesced into a single frequency. As this wave of peace washed over me, I heard the following:

July 5, 2016

All is in perfect balance with the oneness, the divinity of the great universal consciousness.

I took a deep breath as changes coursed through me. I felt my physical body dissolve as I melted into a puddle on Sandra's dining room floor. Although I am unable to explain how I knew this, I had become a radiant pool of liquified quartz crystal.

My watery form sank through the tile floor and into the soil beneath the building. I descended past roots, caves, and underground rivers, permeating layers of Earth's crust until I seeped through the mantle and into our planet's inner core.

I had passed through Earth's strata to become part of Gaia, Mother Earth's spirit. At the center of our planet, Gaia's heart absorbed my essence. Tears streamed down my face as I basked in the divine grace of Mother Earth, and an almost overwhelming love encompassed me.

Moments later, my flowing form rushed back to Earth's surface like a magnificent fountain. As I broke through the final layer of our planet's crust, I swept toward a giant star tetrahedron suspended in midair. My essence poured into its center, flooding into its heart's space.

My fluid shape filled the nooks and crannies of the heart of this divine form, and I realized the star tetrahedron and I were one. I was in its center, yet I had become this majestic form. Metatron spoke:

There are many paths upon the mountain to divinity. I have shown you yet another one. This path begins by letting go and feeling the flow, feeling the connection.

As I scribbled these words in my journal, another transformation occurred. I watched the rotating form revert to its original state. The two tetrahedrons pulled apart to become two triangles that then formed the single diamond that had entered my forehead during the first class.

I experienced an extraordinary shift in perspective that defied logical explanation. My vision widened, and my consciousness expanded well beyond its already stretched margins. I wafted in boundless space, and an immediate full knowing pierced my consciousness like lightning strikes. I realized time and space are one.

Time is different than what I had thought. It is an infinite field with millions of interlocking wheels. I had fallen into a river of endlessness, and its current had carried me to another realm, another dimension I never knew existed.

Layers of my life peeled away, and I felt my existence become smaller than a grain of sand from a gigantic hourglass. The self I had known dissolved into nothingness, for within this vacuum, there is all. There is nowhere I am not, for I am everywhere. There is nothing that I am not, for I am everything.

As I floated in this sacred abyss of no space or time, a hand reached forth to give me something. I accepted the gift and as I examined it, my breath quickened at its beauty. It was a wand; its stem resembled bark of a birch tree, but its luminosity revealed it was made of light. A large bejeweled gem adorned its tip; it was the crystalline diamond from the classes that had become the foundation of the star tetrahedron.

I gave my heartfelt thanks, for I knew I had received another tool for my consciousness-awareness toolbox. This etheric wand represented the transformation of a two-dimensional rhombus into a spinning star tetrahedron, capable of transporting me to other-dimensional spaces beyond my wildest imaginings.

The words "Keepers of the Light" dropped into my awareness, and I immediately knew this represented a congregation of divine beings that included Metatron. In ways I did not know, I understood these beings were part of the sacred nature of these shapes. Within the heart of the two pyramids lies ancient wisdom, protected by Metatron. I heard the following:

The stars are the activation keys to this sacred awareness.

I thought of the forms I had interacted with through the classes, and I understood ancient wisdom lies within the center of the star tetrahedron, that zero point where Metatron resides. It's where the magic occurs.

Stars as activation keys stated the obvious. It had begun with stars that had morphed into various shapes, and I had not realized until now the star tetrahedron's two-dimensional form is a Star of David, a symbol of the union of heaven and Earth.

The final Metatron class took place on July 26. I gathered my belongings and headed to the garage. Summer was winding down, and I had just returned from two programs at Monroe Institute in Virginia: Out of Body Intensive and Journey to Happiness. Both courses helped me integrate the newly found energies from Metatron. I returned to Florida and was ready for another archangel encounter.

I entered Sandra's home and prepared my journal for the final class. As Lee began the angel wash, I closed my eyes and settled into my chair. Within seconds, I found myself inside the life-sized star tetrahedron that had become a fixture in these classes.

The energy from the angel wash appeared to jump-start the star tetrahedron; the tips from both pyramids began to glow. A narrow line of energy streaked around the form's perimeter, connecting the pyramidal caps like dot-to-dot artwork and illuminating its frame with star-like brilliance lit by otherworld radiance.

The frame pulsed, and without warning, bolts of light streaked toward the center of the star tetrahedron, restarting its heart more efficiently than a defibrillator. The center of this sacred design glowed; its zero-point mechanism had returned to life.

The two tetrahedrons began to move. The upper rotated in

one direction with the lower taking the opposite course. While this occurred, the me in the vision floated in silence, merely waiting. Metatron spoke the following:

July 26, 2016

We have liftoff, guided by your heart, in conjunction with intent from your higher self and your angels.

As I stopped writing to wipe my tears, something shifted. My body became lighter until I lifted like the iridescent spheres from a child's bubble wand. As I wafted in this silence, I looked down. My fellow meditation travelers were also drifting upward.

We flew higher; celestial energy gusted and swirled around me, eddying across the star-quilted night sky. We were on this journey together, floating toward source and the divine. The message continued:

This is where the magic happens, for within this divine energy space is the energy of hope, of gratitude, of love. The frequency is in perfect alignment for healing. Sit in this divine open space of magnificence. Let not your heart be troubled for you have come home. We hold you in our arms. You, the most precious and divine soul, we welcome you home.

Were the others aware of what was occurring? I suspected they were not, yet that did not diminish my experience. I drifted in a space of infinite beauty and wonder. Time seemed to stand still as I glided toward a heavenly expanse just beyond my reach.

I would have happily remained in this mystical space had Sandra not called us back. The final exercises blurred past me. The last activity connected us to the spiritual nature of all physical life on our marvelous planet. Undulating swells of heat flowed from my feet to the top of my head, wrapping me in a cocoon of energy. My heart pounded when I realized I was still inside the star tetrahedron. Yet I knew I was safe.

My muscles relaxed, and I sank deep into the muffled enclosure of the cocoon. The swirling motion at the top of my head slipped to a point just below my shoulders. The chrysalis peeled back, freeing me while leaving a brilliant collection of light where my physical body had been. Metatron spoke:

This is your true self, your essence. Shine forth, Dear One, for others to see. Shine forth and be a beacon for others to follow this sacred path back to the oneness of all.

Tears spilled on the pages of my journal as I struggled to write these profound words. This experience was a turning point for me. Each class had brought me further down this path of the divine, and that progression had led me to this singular moment.

A cloud lifted and understanding emerged. I had connected with Metatron through the star tetrahedron, allowing me to step into the unknown realms of the nonphysical, but this was different. As I took a breath, I savored the taste of peace and serenity.

I was changing. My body felt lighter, and an understanding rose from the center of my chest. Like the fragile surface of a bubble bursting, the parameters of my physical body exploded, leaving nothing. I transformed into light, piercing shrouds of existence like sun through dense fog.

For a brief moment in time, I had transcended, and I existed in a sea of all-knowingness. I was aware of myself as I had been thousands of years before and thousands of years to come. I was everything.

The instant passed as quickly as it had begun, and I realized Metatron had been responsible for sharing this unforgettable moment with me. He had allowed me to glimpse the *sacred path back to the oneness of all*. I cannot begin to understand why this had happened to me, but I gave my heartfelt thanks for the privilege of this marvelous experience.

My moment of transcendence had occurred during the last exercise of the final class. There had been a slow progression building to this point in time, but I was ready to seek the larger picture. It was time to find meaning in these experiences that had occurred over these past two months.

The door to discovery was open. As a psychologist, I had learned the benefits of remaining neutral in novel situations. Too much beforehand knowledge could frontload future messages or experiences, so I waited until the classes ended before conducting research.

Unlike communications from other nonphysical friends, Metatron's messages were often brief. As the classes progressed, I realized I would not be relying solely on Metatron's spoken word; I also needed to consider my often curious and surprising interactions with nonphysical geometric forms. I found myself engaging within a nebulous whirlwind of images and experiences involving triangles, circles, diamonds, pyramids, and star tetrahedrons.

I had dipped my toe in the vast realm of the unknown, into dimensions not perceivable with my physical senses. My essence had disappeared into a formless body of energy that was all-knowing. I had floated in the timeless space of the nonphysical, but what did all this mean? I knew the wisdom of Metatron lay embedded within the languid rhythm of these visions, and I had the daunting task to interpret them.

There was much to learn, but first things first: who was Archangel Metatron? I set my cup of freshly brewed coffee on the desk and turned on my MacBook to start searching. Mystical Mind Angelic Heart's website described Metatron as an archangel who is known as the Angel of Ascension.[20] Some believe he had lived on Earth as the Biblical prophet and scribe, Enoch. I smiled when I saw a statement describing Metatron as a "great ally for writers," especially those who seek spiritual truths. I could certainly check that box.

A paragraph detailing Metatron's association with sacred geometric shapes caught my eye. Most of my experiences had involved a star tetrahedron, so that was a great place to begin. Within seconds of entering "star tetrahedron" in Google Images' search bar, hundreds of pyramidal pictures filled my computer screen.

The first image I clicked took me to Star of David's home page, where I learned about this intertwining double pyramid shape that had played such a significant part in the Metatron classes.[21] The website referred to the star tetrahedron as a merkaba. I had heard this name before but where?

A search of my online journal answered my question. During the Metatron meditation on June 7, intersecting beams of light had encompassed my body, placing me inside a crucifix of energy. Metatron had described the center of this cross of light as *the foundation of the merkaba*. I gleaned from the message that merkaba was another name for a star tetrahedron, and I had vowed to research it later.

Seeing the name again piqued my interest. It was time to open the door for discovery. Merkaba. Star tetrahedron. Regardless of the name, piece by piece and exercise by exercise, this majestic figure had evolved. It was obviously associated with Metatron, but I needed a deeper dive to learn more.

---

20 https://mysticalmindangelicheart.wordpress.com/all-about-archangels/archangel-metatron/

21 https://starofdavidsite.wordpress.com/category/double-pyramid-star-of-david/

Returning to Star of David's website, I discovered the star tetrahedron decreases source energy into the physical realm and serves to invoke the "as above, so below" concept. That sounded familiar. Not for the first time, searching my online journal yielded answers.

I located the May 31 message where Metatron described the equator separating the tetrahedrons as *a division between as above and so below*. The star tetrahedron brings higher vibrational energies into physicality through this equatorial space. I was amazed how this research matched the messages from Metatron.

Although these congruent findings fascinated me, I wasn't surprised by the connections. I had learned that truth is like pieces of a mosaic, and often the complete picture is not revealed until all components fall in place.

Once I started down this rabbit hole of researching Metatron, it was difficult to stop as, layer by layer, each Internet click brought more meaning to my experiences. An image I discovered on Crystal Links' homepage stunned me. My spiritual investigation had paid off.

As my eyes fixed on the image, I collapsed into my chair and gasped. How could this be? Staring mutely at the monitor, I nodded and began to grin. I was glaring at a star tetrahedron superimposed over da Vinci's Vitruvian Man.[22] How well I remember the initial Metatron class when I had transformed into that exact figure.

I gave silent thanks for the wisdom to postpone research until the classes had ended. Over the years, I had become accustomed to exploring the outer edges of human consciousness, experiencing events I couldn't explain. Yet I never expected to verify details of these logic-defying adventures through my research. It left me feeling bewildered, speechless.

---

22 https://www.crystalinks.com/merkabah.html

Finding this image fascinated me, and I wanted to stay in the moment to savor its discovery. I saved my document and closed my computer. I couldn't think of a better way to contemplate this finding than a stroll along the Gulf of Mexico. I retrieved my large-brimmed hat, slipped on a long-sleeved sun-proof shirt, grabbed my sunglasses, and took off toward the beach.

I've often used beach walks to decompress, relax, and contemplate the mysteries of life. As I step on the warm sand and feel the gentle waters lap at my feet, all worries and concerns drop away. With each footstep, the incoming waves wash away any traces of my path.

The tide sweeps away my history, and with my previous steps erased, I'm firmly grounded in the now. My only footprints are those in my present moment, and I live within that instant, step by step. As I place one foot in front of the other, with no thoughts of my destination, I drift into a space that allows magic to happen.

I don't dwell in the past or ponder the future, for I know within my heart that I am where I need to be. I breathe a little deeper, smile a little broader, and my life feels purposeful. I go with the flow.

When I recognized the similarities between my beach walk and my spiritual connections, I chuckled. When I exist only within the present moment, all thoughts sail away like dry leaves on an autumn's wind. Within this moment of now, my awareness expands and allows me to step into the energy field connecting me to these divine beings.

After my half-hour walk, I felt refreshed and renewed. I came home, had a bite for lunch, then returned to the task of finding meaning to the Metatron classes; I especially wanted to learn more about the word "merkaba."

In less than five minutes, large pieces of the puzzle fell into place. Ancient Symbols' website revealed "mer" means light, "ka" means spirit, and "ba" means body.[23] It represents the union of spirit with body that is "surrounded by counter-rotating fields of light."

The star tetrahedron had been a permanent fixture in my experiences, evolving and ripening until it had awakened. During the third class, its two pyramidal halves began to spin in opposite directions, matching the description of the "counter-rotating fields of light" from Ancient Symbols' website. I was tucked inside this majestic form, a literal manifestation of the translation of the word "merkaba." United as one, the star tetrahedron and I rocketed through deep space as if in a wormhole.

But was there a difference between a merkaba and a star tetrahedron? The answer was on Crystal Link's homepage.[24] The counter-moving pyramids had energized the star tetrahedron, transforming it into a vehicle of light, a merkaba.

I had been in the center of a star tetrahedron when its two spinning pyramids catapulted me into space. At that point, as I accelerated through a velvety dark sky dotted with galaxies, I was no longer in a star tetrahedron; it had become a merkaba.

My head spun with this knowledge. I knew that somehow through this sacred shape, I had dipped into the waters of the divine and traveled beyond time and space. It had served as a chariot of light that carried me to ever-expanding realms of existence that were outside the three-dimensional world I had known.

Learning the merkaba was a vehicle of light added clarity to the extraordinary experiences I'd had with this shape. Everything was beginning to make sense. It seemed one discovery led to another, and more pieces of the puzzle fell into place. Learning the star tetrahedron was used for travel made sense, but I wondered why that had surprised me.

---

23 https://www.ancient-symbols.com/symbols-directory/merkaba.html

24 https://www.crystalinks.com/merkabah.html

It was apparent. I had even compared my travels to the machine in the movie *Contact* that carried Dr. Eleanor Arroway into another dimension. I had also envisioned myself floating on a beam of light as I slipped into the rotating star tetrahedron. But the most obvious missed connection occurred in the final class.

Metatron had stated *We have liftoff, guided by your heart in conjunction with intent from your higher self and your angels.* With those words, while tucked securely in the star tetrahedron, I drifted upward. From a place high above Sandra's living room, I had looked down in time to see the other participants also rise in their merkabas.

This last message and experience clearly depicted this divine form's vehicular nature, yet I had remained blissfully unaware. My obtuseness must have pushed my guides and angels into overtime to help me make this connection.

I delved deeper into the research and encountered sacred geometry, figures with deep metaphysical meanings that have existed since ancient times. Even Plato had recognized these forms as a link between the spiritual and the physical.

As I skimmed through multiple webpages, I discovered sacred geometry's connection to something called Metatron's Cube. In an article entitled Archangel Metatron's Cube in Sacred Geometry on Learn Religions' website, Whitney Hopler reported Metatron uses this mystical cube to connect to our world.[25] Hopler said Metatron's Cube contains the geometric shapes of creation that form all physical matter, including the pyramids that form the star tetrahedron, the merkaba.

A merkaba embedded in Metatron's Cube? I shook my head in disbelief at the finding. Once again, the after-the-fact research confirmed the connection between my geometric-laden

---

25 Hopler, Whitney. "Archangel Metatron's Cube in Sacred Geometry." Learn Religions, Jun. 5, 2019, learnreligions.com/archangel-metatrons-cube-in-sacred-geometry-124293

experiences and Metatron.

Why were these shapes considered sacred? It was time to unwrap the veils of mystery surrounding them. An article entitled *What is Sacred Geometry?* by Martina Coogan on Modern Mystery School's website indicated sacred geometry connects all creation. Coogan stated these forms represent patterns that weave the world into existence, explaining all that is. Not only are these shapes found throughout nature from the molecular structure of a grain of sand to the foundations of galaxies but in the "complex, all-encompassing marvels like Metatron's Cube." They are the universal mathematical templates found everywhere.

I beamed when Coogan mentioned Leonardo da Vinci and his Vitruvian man. She reported da Vinci was an initiate of the Mystery School, and he had completed his 1490 Vitruvian Man drawing using an aspect of sacred geometry called the Golden Ratio.

Connecting the dots between sacred geometry, a merkaba in Metatron's cube, and da Vinci's Vitruvian Man pushed against the edges of my beliefs about life. More puzzle pieces locked into place as the investigation verified and articulated what I had experienced but had not known at the time.

Each search engine hit made me realize what I believe had little to do with truth. Truth is rarely straightforward. It seems to be fluid, changing sometimes day by day, dependent upon perspective.

Yet through this process of seeking answers, I grew closer to my truth. I realized these geometric designs connected me to both the spiritual and physical worlds. Perhaps Plato was right when he said sacred geometry linked heaven and Earth.

My spiritual path was not so much a journey but a discovery of what was already there. French novelist Marcel Proust stated, "The real voyage of discovery consists not in seeking new landscapes, but in having new eyes." I had not sought the experiences with the classes' sacred geometric designs, yet the research's explanation offered a new view, a different perspective. Observing my experiences through this new set of lenses helped explain what I thought was inexplicable.

But it was more than just a new perspective. My after-the-fact research confirmed what might be public information in some circles, but it was new to me. Metatron's chariot of light had carried me to ever-expanding realms of existence that were outside the three-dimensional world I had known. But learning of his connection to the merkaba through firsthand experiences spoke to a higher, more universal truth.

My adventures were like fragments of evidence that whispered just below the surface of what I thought was my ordinary life. Truth is sometimes mysterious and elusive, but like a light that pierces the fog, it shines on which path to follow.

These whisperings transformed and revolutionized me as they broke through my consciousness; I soon found myself walking an unknown path. Each new discovery pushed me beyond limits that had previously defined me. I learned that truths discovered are uniquely my own, and I had not only stepped into the role of an explorer in the outer edges of human consciousness, but I had embraced it.

CHAPTER 11: WHISPERS

My experiences with the seraphim and Archangel Metatron changed the face of my interactions with angels. Their messages were no longer their primary means of communication, but I never expected the twists that occurred in 2019 and its unforeseen impact in 2020.

Angels surround us, but they don't usually interfere with day-to-day activities without a request. We can call on their assistance by prayer, thought, or even a simple wish. It's the intent, often unspoken, that draws them into our energy fields. Sacred gatherings serve as powerful and open invitations for them to intervene. Angels had communicated with me numerous times during meditations, but 2019 brought surprising changes in this mystical courtship of consciousness.

These transformations evolved over a series of five meditations. When I took down my shingle as a psychologist in June 2018, I replaced IEP and Section 504 Accommodation Plan meetings with activities that lifted my spirit. Recurrent events in my post-retirement schedule included Friday's morning meditations at Goddess I Am in Naples and the twice-monthly Crystal Bowl Meditation and Energy Healing at Church of Spiritual Light in Fort Myers.

Over the past few years, I had learned to associate images with specific angelic presences: purple mist with seraphim, merkaba with Metatron, and pastel pink and green ribbons of energy with most other angels. But in mid-March and April 2019, this repertoire of telltale and predictable symbols expanded to include vivid and even more far-fetched imagery.

Events can unfold in such a manner that overnight you find yourself seeking answers to questions not yet asked. Uncanny shards of knowledge hide metaphysical secrets that you've only begun to glimpse, yet over time, scraps of experience fuse to present a bigger picture.

It began during a morning meditation at Goddess I Am. I arrived early and settled in my chair. When I dug into my purse for my favorite blue pen, I pulled out a red one. I was puzzled; I hadn't used a red pen in years, so how could it be the only writing instrument in this small purse I'd carried for months?

I pulled off the cap and jotted March 15 at the top of my journal's page. The date made me think of the soothsayer's line, "Beware of the Ides of March," in William Shakespeare's play *Julius Caesar*. This thought must have been my cosmic heads-up about the message because seconds later, the following words glided into my awareness:

March 15, 2019

Beware. Beware as we surround you with loving energy, with divine love.

Moments before the meditation began, shop owner Beth Brown-Rinella offered the participants a spritz from an essential oil mixture. I couldn't help but smile when my shoulder neighbor handed me the cobalt blue bottle. With print large enough for my eyes to see in the dimly lit room, I saw its label, "Love." With the smile still painted on my face, I looked down. There it was again, but in red ink; it was the last word I had penned in my journal.

When we began the meditation with a few deep breaths, my first inhalation brought a flood of valentines from above. As I colored the glittering whirlwind of tiny hearts in my journal, I realized my ink was the exact shade of red from my mind's eye. Was this why the pen had mysteriously materialized at the bottom of my purse?

The room was alive with dazzling red hearts, falling and covering the floor like autumn leaves. When the shower of valentines stopped, the river of hearts rushed down an opening that had formed in the center of the room.

A gurgling sound caught my attention. Within seconds, the crimson flow reversed direction, bubbling to the ceiling, then cascaded over us like a fountain. These waves of red circled our bodies. As they looped back into the fountain, the spinning energy encased us in a torus field of hearts.

Feelings of comfort and protection enveloped me, intensifying like a tidal wave of unconditional compassion. I had never associated red hearts with the angelic realm, but this energy was unmistakable. Without a doubt, the angels had arrived. The message continued:

The circle represents wholeness, timelessness, solidarity. Embrace this living, dynamic representation of love.

I knew angels were in our presence, but this imagery was different from anything I'd ever experienced with them. The vision shifted, and this unusual scenario became even more bizarre as the toroidal ring rose a few feet off the floor. While in midair, it shrank and then transformed into a tambourine that floated at my eye level. It slowly wobbled back and forth, sending gentle jingles across the room. The vibrations increased, strengthening the ring of hearts and summoning divine energy into our space.

Stepping forth from the center of this amplifying ring of love came a divine being of light, an angel. As I welcomed her, a messenger spoke:

She lives within. Open your heart to welcome her more fully into your life. Dance to the music within. Call forth the energy of divinity, love, and compassion. Bring this energy into your heart.

As you breathe, be mindful, and allow the compassion of the angels to enter into your divine space. Tap into the connection of our realm. Let the love that surrounds you enter your divine self. Allow that love to guide you as you traverse the path of life.

We are always around, awaiting your call for aid. Be mindful of this and see us as trusted friends. We look over you with the love and compassion a mother has for her beloved child. Know that we are here, simply awaiting your call.

With these words, the vision changed. As if on cue, the tambourine made a 180-degree midair turn. I felt a discernable shift of energy, and the soft lyrical jingles became a jarring cacophony of clangs and clatters as it moved above my head. The clamor and racket shocked me; the noise was so incongruent with the gentle music that had welcomed the angel into our space.

The tambourine danced around me, and its vibrations reverberated down my spine as it circled me from head to toe. The sound shattered parts of my energy body; dark pieces broke loose and drifted from me like smoldering ashes. I realized this represented old, stale energy that was no longer useful. The message continued:

Call upon the divine to enter your heart. Release that which no longer serves you. Know that you have the power, for it lies within. You are not alone; we are here to guide you. We are here to assist. Call upon us, and we shall answer. Use this spirit tambourine as a portal to access our dimension.

The imagery of a spirit tambourine made from a flood of crimson valentines surprised me, but it shined a light on the purpose of the heart. It is through this magnificent organ that we release old energies to make way for new. It is a path to transcendence. The heart becomes an interdimensional portal, for these higher vibrational frequencies allow passage into the angelic realms of love and compassion.

The angels indicated the spirit tambourine, made by heart energy, was a tool to step into a vortex. Over the years, I'd learned to recognize nonphysical portals and vortices in places I would consider sacred such as churches, mosques, synagogues, meditation centers, and settings in nature. Yet I had overlooked what was with me at all times—my heart.

The angels were empowering us, as humans, to use our hearts as portals, for this is where divinity lives. Through our hearts, we can seek sacred refuge. A sense of deep appreciation welled up inside me as I welcomed this new tool in my awakening-of-consciousness toolbox.

Three days later, I attended another meditation that made the whirlwind of hearts imagery pale in comparison. Due to seasonal traffic, it took over an hour to make the 30-mile trip to Fort Myers for the Crystal Bowl Meditation and Energy Healing at Church of Spiritual Light.

After registering, I headed to my favorite place. It's close to one of the few lights that remain on during the meditation, making it an ideal location to journal my experiences. I settled in, adding extra pillows and blankets to my cot. Although the event wouldn't start for another twenty minutes, I felt the extraordinary energy of the angels approach me.

I closed my eyes and sighed deeply as a set of massive wings wrapped around my body. A few seconds later, I found myself standing in a deeply wooded forest. In the blink of an eye, I had gone from the Church of Spiritual Light to this mystical woodland.

I began to walk a path that led deeper into the woods. A light breeze lifted my hair. I traveled in silence with my eyes on the ground, and every once in a while, a ray of sunlight broke through the branches to light golden spots on the path. I was alone in the stillness with nothing but the rustling of leaves around me.

As I topped a hill, I found myself standing at a fork in the path. Which way should I turn? I felt as if I had dropped in the middle of Robert Frost's poem, *The Road Not Taken*, and I had to make a choice. The message began:

March 18, 2019

Which is your path?

As that question reverberated in my thoughts, I looked around at the vision still playing in my mind's eye. I wanted to remember the details; it felt so real. The musty, damp scent of pine trees permeated the air as I walked the path that had beckoned me. Dry leaves crunched beneath my bare feet, but within minutes, it changed to a soft, compact cushion of moss. As I raised my hand to brush the wind-blown hair from my face, the distant sound of a babbling brook caught my attention. I recognized this as a sign from the angels, so I turned toward that faint sound that whispered to me.

Guidance beckoned me toward an even quieter path, so I veered from my current course. As I followed the trail down a small incline, I found the source of the melodious calling: a shallow, crystal-clear stream that invited me to enter.

I stepped into the gurgling waters that bubbled and splashed over its rough bed. I lifted a couple of its smooth rocks and immediately knew the rivers of time had changed these once-rough stones to their now-smooth texture. Was this an analogy for me? Would following the right path smooth my rough edges?

As these thoughts entered my mind, I merged with the bubbling spring. Like a leaf floating atop the water, the current carried me, and I realized I was no longer human; I had become the rippling brook. The message continued:

Come, come. Allow. Rest your weary bones in these deep, relaxing waters. Let it replenish your soul. Allow divine grace to flow through your cells. Allow these waters to lead you through the paths of righteousness.

As the angelic messenger spoke these words, I maintained a state of allowing and agreed for these divine waters to carry me on this unknown yet somehow familiar path. I was literally going with the flow.

I looked around and marveled at the abundance of nature. Birds fluttered overhead, and their harmonious sounds permeated the air. A deer approached the brook and drank, replenishing its body with these clean, radiant waters. It was nature at its purest, with no humans to break the tranquility.

The stream flowed through the woods, absorbing other bodies of water that had rushed to join it, and soon it became a small river. I remained part of it, moving ever so swiftly to some undisclosed destination. Although the waters rushed toward places unknown, I trusted. I was at peace. As the river coursed through the woodland, I heard the words "River of Light."

Immediately, the waterway lifted into the sky, and my conscious awareness exploded. Images flickered in front of me. I had a glimpse of a large brown bear and heard the words "Ursa Major." Stars blurred past me at warp speed as the river burst through its banks, flooding into deep space before pooling in a giant void stretched between stars.

The stillness within this abyss of silence shattered when a form whizzed past me. My essence bolted upward from the River of Light to catch it. I connected with this nebulous shape and realized I had become part of a winged horse shooting through the cosmos.

The cosmic horse continued flying through the inky skies, drawing more celestial objects into its wake. With no warning, my essence dissolved, and I merged with the heavens. I became the light, and I was free from my physical body that had bound me to my three-dimensional life on Earth. I was everything. This was my source; the angels had brought me home.

For the second time in three days, vivid imagery had transported me to new levels of understanding. These adventures were different from previous angelic connections, yet not unlike the experiential escapades I'd had with Metatron and the seraphim.

It's true; I'd experienced moments of unity and transcendence, but I struggled to understand why. Perhaps this would be the wave of the future for me with experiences overshadowing the messages. Had these snippets of wholeness and perfection altered my energy body? Were these higher vibrations changing me? Did each visit to the angelic realm help me in my day-to-day life?

Although I did not understand why things had changed, I knew these events were profound. I had no answers, but in the back of my mind, I hoped one day I would discover the mystery behind them.

Several days after the meditation, I transcribed my hand-written notes. As I typed the details in a word document, I yearned for more information. There was a lot to unpack: hearing Ursa Major, seeing a large bear, and becoming a winged horse, all while zooming through the cosmos on the River of Light.

I began with Ursa Major. NASA Science's website revealed

this constellation's common name is Great Bear.[26] Had this been the bear I had seen? From there, I discovered the brightest stars from the Great Bear form the bowl of the Big Dipper; this must have been the void I had seen that stretched between stars. It was the source of the River of Light as it flowed to Earth and returned on its cosmic journey. I also learned the Big Dipper's bowl is in direct alignment with the Great Square of Pegasus, the winged horse of my vision.[27]

I smiled at the synchronicities between the research findings and the elements of the vision. When results dovetail perfectly, I realize it's a harmonious match, verifying information that had been unknown when it occurred. This is part of the magic with the nonphysical world. When you least expect it, the experiences you have coincide with the truth.

My take-away from this meditation was learning to relinquish my resistance. I needed to go with the flow and have faith in what I received. These were significant steps in the spiritual process, and they had enriched my experiences in this journey called life.

Four days later, the third in this series of angel communications occurred. While I sat outside Goddess I Am waiting for the doors to open for Friday's morning meditation, I heard the whispers of the angels. I grabbed my favorite blue pen to write the message. It seemed to be a continuation of the previous communique about choosing a path. The following words flowed into my awareness:

March 22, 2019

The road to peace begins with you, so step gently on the path of life. Let each footstep mean something. It need not be monumental; it just needs to be purposeful and with heart.

Let your heart guide you. Take each step without knowing

26 https://science.nasa.gov/big-dipper-over-pyramid-mountain

27 www.constellation-guide.com/great-square-of-pegasus/

what the next step will be. This is trust. This is guidance.

Know that within your heart is a beacon. It is a connection to angels, a connection to source. Find the stillness inside so that you may hear the whispers upon the wind that guide you on the path of wisdom, the path of love, the path of the sacred.

My awareness pulled away, and I found myself with a panoramic perspective over North America. Lights flickered across our nation's night sky, and I zoomed for a closer look at the brighter ones. These were clusters of lights at meditation centers, mosques, synagogues, churches, and other places of universal love.

As I drew closer, I realized the light was like nothing I had ever seen. What I had witnessed from above had not come from these sacred places; it had come from the people: a living, radiant glow. The message continued:

These bright souls are bringing more light into the Earth plane. With each step they take, they help bring us to the path of the sacred. There will be a tipping point. When that occurs, it will catapult your lovely planet into another dimensional space where we will be awaiting all of humanity with our open arms.

Evolution is a slow-moving process that introduces change into all living things, including Mother Earth. The messengers had told me before, as Gaia transforms, she brings all of her inhabitants with her. This new communication, however, indicated there would be a spiritual tipping point for people. When this occurs, it will provide the final push for our planet to enter a new dimensional space.

This message took on more significance fourteen months later. With my final review of the manuscript before sending it to editors, my breath quickened when I saw the angel's words foretelling a tipping point for Earth.

As I write these words in May 2020, we find ourselves in various stages of lockdown across the globe due to COVID-19 that became a pandemic earlier this year. Pandemics know no borders, storming shores across the world and throwing humanity into anxiety and alarm as our daily lives change overnight. For the lucky ones, telecommuting replaces in-office jobs. For others, unemployment rises to levels not seen in the United States since the Great Depression of the 1930s. Parents become teachers as schools implement distance learning.

Fear runs amuck as the monumental loss of life increases daily, compounded by the threat of economic collapse. We have entered an unparalleled era with no roadmaps to navigate the waters of these unprecedented times. We are left to our own devices to survive—or are we?

Yet one year before the World Health Organization declared the novel coronavirus outbreak a global pandemic, a cosmic heads-up had infiltrated my awareness. Viewing this March 2019 message in 2020 offers me a different perspective; it gives me hope as I realize we aren't alone. The angels are here to help us negotiate these new times.

COVID-19 is a wakeup call for humanity; it offers us a reset, a do-over. As our planet creeps toward a spiritual tipping point, opportunities arise for us to reinvent ourselves. When we step into the higher vibrations of the new Earth, what will we do differently?

We have the chance to look beyond our limited perspectives and see humanity as one. We are global citizens of a world without borders. Will we be able to embrace the unity that surrounds us?

As Earth transcends, the veils between the dimensions will thin, allowing us to glimpse at our true nature. For those with the ears to hear and the eyes to see, perhaps for the first time in our lives, we'll be able to communicate with the nonphysical realms of angels and guides. As we merge with these new dimensional spaces, our angels are cheering for us, welcoming us to these higher frequencies.

This global pandemic has brought us to a tipping point, and we are teetering on the precipice. The path we've traveled our entire lives has vanished. I now realize the last two messages foretold where we are now—we stand at the fork in the road, and we must make choices.

Will we heed angelic advice to listen to the wisdom of our hearts? Will we allow the angels to guide us into this new territory of spirit? Will the lessons learned assist us in this new Earth, or will we resist the change, clawing our way back to our old lives? The choices are ours to make.

I leave you to ponder these questions as we return to the 2019 message:

Be ye one with the divine spirit. Trust what your heart tells you, for you are loved beyond measure. You are love. Let that divine spark in your heart grow and fan its embers with the winds of love so that others may see the divinity within.

An intuitive thought came to me, and I understood those individual and clusters of lights I had seen were divine sparks. Each person is born with a sacred light that burns brightly in their hearts. Depending on how we react to the trials and tribulations of life, those sparks can dim. Our day-to-day challenges often lead us away from our life's real purpose, and the further we drift, the fainter our divine sparks appear.

In my mind's eye, I saw a table lamp with a single lit bulb. One at a time, a series of thin scarves covered the light. Although I knew the bulb maintained its brightness, its radiance diminished with each added layer.

I understood the analogy. As we walk our paths of life, we make choices, and those choices determine our luminosity.

Engaging with lower vibrations of fear and anger will cover our divine sparks, while higher frequencies of love and gratitude allow our luminescence to shine. I grinned at this literal depiction of enlightenment.

If we navigate a path of wisdom, our lights shine brighter, and we become beacons for others who are searching. We see the collective benefit when groups come together in the powerhouses around our Earth, those sacred places where like-minded people gather to celebrate a higher power. We become more luminous and heart-based, and as our lights shine from within, we call others to join us.

I received many messages over the next nine days, but these intense angelic experiences interested me the most. The dramatic imagery weighed on my mind. These encounters had taken me by surprise, and I was trying to make sense of them. I decided a beach walk would be a perfect opportunity to clear my thoughts to see if new insights might arrive.

It was spring in Naples, and the daytime's low eighties temperatures had dropped twenty degrees during the night. The weather was perfect for an early morning walk, so I grabbed my go-cup of coffee and headed out the door before seven. I slipped off my shoes to stroll along the sandy beach of the Gulf of Mexico. The water lapping at my feet felt warm compared to the chilly air.

As I walked, I contemplated the recent angelic messages. As much as I desired to accept the last three experiences at face value, my analytical training as a psychologist wouldn't let me. I wanted more. I struggled to find a pattern; I needed these experiences to fit into a logical, sequential order, but they didn't.

Little did I know May 2020 would bring the insight I sought. As I view these events through the eyes of a world ensnared by coronavirus, the pattern emerges. These messages and experiences had built the foundation for our survival in a post-pandemic world, giving us the roadmap into a new Earth as we awaken spiritually.

I finished my walk and busied myself with clearing my to-do list and preparing for the week ahead. My grandfather's clock chimed noon as I finished my household chores. Miss Nancy, the girls' nanny, and I alternated days babysitting, and this was my day to pick up Shalane. I had just enough time to clean up and drive to the preschool.

Rivers of sunlight flooded through my windows, reminding me to grab my sunhat. In a few hours, I would need it for the walk to the end of the block to meet Lorelai's bus. I got in my car and headed to school. Within twenty-minutes, Shalane and I were on our way to her house. After a quick snack and taking Loki on a short walk, we lost ourselves in the pure blissful fantasy of play that comes so naturally to prekindergarten students.

Shalane was modeling her new Easter shoes from Miss Nancy when my iPhone alerted me it was time to head to the bus stop. I buckled the princess in the stroller and walked to the end of the block. We took refuge from the sun under the leafy canopy of a single mahogany tree adjacent to the stop sign.

As the bus rounded the corner at the end of the street, Shalane began to wave. The long yellow school bus arrived, its old brakes grinding to a halt. Lorelai was the second to exit. She descended the steep steps and ran toward me yelling, "Nana!" As she wrapped her long, thin arms around me, I choked back tears. Oh, the love of a grandchild!

I passed the baton to Cassie and Dan a few hours later. Glancing at my watch told me there was enough time to travel to Fort Myers for the Crystal Bowl Meditation and Energy Healing at Church of Spiritual Light. The traffic was relatively light, and I arrived with time to spare.

After checking in, I entered the familiar room of cots surrounding crystal bowls and headed to my favorite spot to prepare for the meditation. No sooner had I nestled into a comfortable position when I heard and saw the word "Faith." I felt the unmistakable presence of an angel. Tears sprang from my eyes as this celestial being spoke:

April 1, 2019

Have faith in your journey of life. Know your truth is found in the steps you take—one at a time, leading you to your truth. Each person's path is individual, and only their steps can lead them down this sacred path of truth.

Let go of any thoughts that distract you. Bring forth goodness. Allow it to permeate your physical body, your energy body, and your soul.

Faith. The energy of faith falls like a silent snow upon the grasses of Earth, covering all with a divine blanket of purity. Let your body sink in it. Bathe in this timeless, ageless wisdom.

Although I was mindful of my surroundings at the church, my perspective changed. From a darkened sky, I observed myself standing in a silent, snow-covered plain below; I was alone but not afraid.

I watched the other-me fall backward in slow motion. My heart raced as my body dropped into this artic abyss; the snow beckoned me to travel deeper. As I sank, snow toppled over me until I was completely covered.

Within this darkness, the purity of the white snow encompassed me. I felt nothing but love and protection as I sank into this deep snowdrift of whispering silence. An odd sensation shattered my peace, and I dissolved into the consciousness of the snow. The me I thought I was had disappeared, but my essence remained.

The observer-me detected movement. As I glanced up, a large snowy owl glided across the velvety sky in silent meandering circles above the snow-filled plain where the other-me had recently stood. I smiled. I had seen this spectacular bird three and one-half months before in this same room. The arrival of the snowy owl could only mean one thing—the Angel of Peace had returned. The message continued:

> *Know ye are one with God, one with Creator, for a divine spark from the Creator's bosom has been placed in your heart.*
>
> *Know your truth. Know your wisdom. Know your unity with all that is. Move as one. Move in silence like the snowy owl who soars above the snow-driven fields: silent, ever so silent as it soaks in the void—that magical darkness of the unmanifested where all things are possible.*

My mid-pandemic perspective understood the significance of the message. Humanity is one, and self-imposed borders cannot alter that fact. How readily we have donned blinders to keep our sights narrow, allowing us to ignore the uncomfortable.

The Angel of Peace tells us to *move as one.* When we recognize the truth of unity, we will see all humanity as brothers and sisters; we will not only survive but thrive. We are global citizens of this grand blue-green planet, and it's not us versus them. As one large family, we can move in unison to manifest what we need as we prepare to enter the new Earth.

The words of the message returned the snowy owl to my mind's eye. Soundless, this magnificent bird pierced the midnight sky like an arrow. The darkness of flight was not of shadow; it was the fertile mystery of a mother's womb, of potential waiting to be birthed upon a new horizon.

I drifted back to late 2018 when I'd first met the Angel of Peace, and I'd seen a snowy owl soaring across a winter's sky with tiny toy churches and houses below. This miniature Victorian village, nestled within the dome of a snow globe, was small enough to fit in my palm. The Angel of Peace had said *We install a globe of love around you and your precious world.* Similar to the current message, the Angel of Peace had called this a time of unity and fullness, comparing it to *a mother ready to birth her child.*

Coming full circle, as spring of 2020 blooms, indeed, we find ourselves deep within the belly of Mother Earth, waiting to be birthed into a new world. Until then, we linger in this magical place where all possibilities exist. We rest, tucked inside our cocoons, awaiting transformation. The message continued:

Have faith, my Love, for guidance is within you. It is like the wisdom of the owl as he sees within the dark void of probabilities and possibilities of the unmanifested world where all things are born.

Viewing this message through a May 2020 lens reinforces the importance of faith. We are not alone as we await the dawning of a new era. The messengers insist this is the time to go inside, but this is not in reference to the current shelter-in-place, stay-at-home, and lockdown orders across our globe. It is time to go within and listen to the wisdom from your heart. Have faith in the guidance of the angels who surround you.

As I scribbled these words in my journal, I returned to the other-me buried deep within the bowels of the snow. My icy tomb began to crack. The surrounding darkness dissolved as I accelerated through the snowdrift. Pushing through the final layer, I rocketed into the atmosphere.

Blinded by the light of acceleration, I sank into the comfort of my closed eyes. When the motion stopped, I could not believe what I saw. I had transformed into a being of light. My spiritual form floated within a vast void of potential, exactly as the message indicated. I was in a place where anything and everything was possible. While in this state of immense bliss, the Angel of Peace continued:

Soar into the darkness, knowing that a supreme connection to the divine guides your inner vision. Float in this mystical, magical space. Allow faith to guide you.

Soaring within a dark, silent void of limitless possibilities, we enter a chrysalis of potential. We can use the time of self-isolation to connect to our inner visions and harness that magic to imagine the world to come as we want to see it, knowing the divine guides it. As we connect with our angels, we begin to manifest our places in the new Earth, knowing we are transcending from the way the world was to what we wish it to be.

Faith. That was the key. The message had begun with that single word, and I realized we needed to trust the whispers of angels as they accompany us through unknown paths that we must tread. Yes, we can be the change we wish to see as we prepare to enter our new Earth, but we're not alone. Our angels and guides are with us.

The next morning while transcribing last night's journal notes, I took a break to check my social media accounts. Two posts from people who had attended the meditation made me grin. Just minutes before driving to Church of Spiritual Light, Sandy had uploaded a picture of a stuffed toy snowy owl. I then noticed a day-old selfie from Reverend Bledsoe holding a replica of Hedwig, Harry Potter's infamous snowy owl.

Snowy owls had manifested online prior to my vision. I nodded and smiled at these findings. It brought me back to the angelic message of faith and knowing that our inner visions link to the divine, but not many see connections between the physical and nonphysical.

Through images of swirling valentines, trips through the cosmos, and snowy owls, the angels spoke of spiritual growth for us individually and collectively. These celestial beings showed me how the power of one could catalyze more. Spiritual strength increases as people gather in sacred places, impacting larger segments of the population.

Many of the angelic messengers spoke of things to come, foretelling events that we see unfolding now. As we retreat to the safety of our homes, it's comforting to know our angels are with us as we seek refuge within.

Eleven days after my snowy owl encounter, the fifth in the series of angel messages arrived, shedding more light on our divine nature.

The morning sun crept into my bedroom window, nudging me from sleep. I got up and prepared my cup of pour-over coffee. I had plenty of time before I'd need to leave for Friday's morning meditation at Goddess I Am. As my grandfather's clock marked the quarter-hour, I gathered my journal, water, and my purse and headed to the car.

As I drove the short distance to the shop, I couldn't help but notice the beauty that surrounded me. Green trees swayed gently in the spring breeze; the golden glow of the bright Florida sunshine bathed the land with warmth and light.

I thought about how perfect life seemed, but then I remembered recent discussions to the contrary. Just a couple of days before, I'd overheard conversations of day-to-day chaos caused by some planetary retrograde status. I didn't understand what that meant, and I certainly didn't feel the same effects as others. My life seemed idyllic.

While stopped at a red light, the subtle nudge of a messenger slipped into my awareness. These familiar vibrations told me it was from the angel realm. I grabbed my phone and recorded the following:

April 12, 2019

Rise above the petty concerns that might surround your day-to-day activities. For this is the true path to enlightenment. It is learning to step into the divine by choice. It is learning to reduce those energy frequencies that bombard you and take you away from your true purpose, your true path in life.

Enlightenment for the modern human is a task that can be achieved by not fighting incoming mal-aligned frequencies but rather learning how to defray and deflect those energies away from your true self.

March forward. March onward. March to the beat of your drum as it connects to higher sources. Feel the beat from the heart of Mother Earth. Look upward. Raise your eyes. Raise your heart. Raise your intentions to higher and loftier goals. Know that ye are one and allow that oneness to guide you on the path of wisdom.

I arrived at the meditation, and immediately things felt off. Within a minute or two, waves of unsettled vibrations washed over me and replaced my peaceful mood with unease. This frenetic whirlwind didn't seem harmful, merely erratic and disquieting. Was this the energy of the planetary retrograde that I had just dismissed as fiction?

We began the meditation by taking several deep breaths. As people exhaled, a milky-white smoky substance left their mouths and wafted to the ceiling. In a fraction of a second, I dissolved, vanishing into this moving mass of clouds. Darkness descended as I slipped through a vortex at the top of the room that launched me into a silent, cosmic void. As I entered the heavens above, I burst into billions of light particles that exploded upward into this magnificent space.

The movement stopped as quickly as it had begun, and the

specks of light sprinkled down and pooled on invisible waves of energy. I had become a raft of golden light, riding on a cosmic ocean like a glittering amoeba.

Multiple tunnels surrounded me, and I intuitively understood they represented different realms of existence or possibilities. I knew I could access any of these, but I chose to float in this sea of nothingness, this sea of everything. Potential surrounded me, just awaiting my intentions to call forth the energies to manifest whatever I sought. I felt at peace, at one with the universe. This was perfection. While swimming in this ocean of serenity, the angels spoke:

Peace be unto you as you come and rest your concerns and problems at our feet. Know that you are loved beyond measure. Know that you are part of a divine plan. Trust that the path will be lighted for you. Release that which does not serve you.

As you enter higher realms of consciousness, feel our presence. Know that we accompany you on this path. Call upon us, for we are here to help you traverse your journey of life.

Once again, a May 2020 perspective shined a different light on the message, offering insight in a time of crisis. The angels show us a path to peace by offering to ease our burdens, and as we realize our part in the divine plan, we feel empowered.

Earth's evolutionary changes are bringing her into a new space; the veil between dimensions is thinning. Trust. Have faith that our angels are here to help us on this journey. As we trust our connections to angels and guides, the paths will become apparent. As we step into the post-pandemic world, the frequencies of our new Earth will allow for closer connections with divine sources, and guidance will be easier to ascertain. It will begin with those with the eyes to see and ears to hear.

This tipping point will begin as small groups of truth-seekers emerge, silently observing through new eyes. As these torchbearers go forth, they will light the path for others to follow. As we step into the higher vibrations of this new world, we will feel the peace that surrounds us. We will see Earth as a living, breathing entity, and we will begin to operate in unity as one. There will be peace on Earth, and it will begin with us.

We returned from the meditation, and the raft of golden glitter swept back through the vortex, like water down a drain. The floating lights hovered above my chair like a helicopter preparing to drop its fragile cargo. I was conflicted, feeling both relief and disappointment as the raft released my consciousness back into my body. With the agility of a hummingbird, the raft of lights veered away, but not before circling the room and sprinkling its luminance on each meditation participant.

Peace and serenity filled the room; gone were the chaotic, unsettled energies from the beginning of the meditation. I took a deep breath and smiled. The angels had said we could step into the divine by choice. When we rise above our petty concerns, we enter a realm of higher vibrations. Within these blissful spaces, we experience unity. We realize we are not our physical bodies; instead, we are part of all there is. We move as one, part of a divine plan.

The angels had told me we begin our lives as humans on Earth by passing through an interdimensional barrier called the veil of forgetfulness. This filtering mechanism allows our expansive nonphysical selves to operate within the denser energies of our planet, but it also wipes our pre-Earth memories.

In spring 2019, the angels foretold of changes in Earth, stating she would experience an upgrade. They reported Earth's vibrations were becoming lighter as the parameters surrounding the world of physicality evolved. One year later, amid a global pandemic, I see these changes in action.

By choice, we can learn to recognize and then deflect negative and low-level energies that bombard us. Diverting those away allows our authentic selves to shine. This small step toward enlightenment is just the beginning. One choice at a time, we lift the veil of forgetfulness, bringing us closer to the angel realm and our divine selves.

When it is time to emerge from our homes, will we recognize sacred connections? Will we follow the angels as they lead us into these unknown territories of a post-pandemic world? The choice is ours.

When we trust and know we are loved and protected by these divine beings, we begin to recognize their presence in our day-to-day lives. When we follow their guidance, hope rises within as we realize the power of our divinity.

We soar through the darkness of night, instinctually guided to wisdom and truth. We move on separate paths, yet knowing we are one with the Creator. We fly with the stealth of the snowy owl, gliding into the sea of potential, of possibilities waiting to be birthed upon the next horizon. In silence, we move into that *magical darkness of the unmanifested where all things are possible.* We rest our concerns at the feet of the angels and know we are part of an inspired design.

I knew the angels had guided my experiences, but suddenly I had an epiphany about the nature of these interactions. Seven years had passed since my spontaneous opening to spirit, and my adventures had become increasingly more transcendent: floating in unmanifested voids, merging with sacred geometric forms, flying through the cosmos, melting into timelessness. Most of these experiences were brief, but they were almost too beautiful to last. My hold on to them was fleeting, but even at that, the briefest of moments can endure a lifetime. Through these experiences, my connections to the nonphysical strengthened as I realized my part in Mother Earth's evolution.

As our planet evolves, she brings us into higher vibrations; little by little, the veil of forgetfulness will fade. When we cross the post-pandemic threshold, we will begin a new path, one where our perceptions will change. We'll begin to see that all dimensions exist simultaneously; they are simply different perspectives of one universal truth: love.

For the first time in my life, I began to understand the power of the heart. Love is the unifying field of everything in time and space. Through this magical portal of the heart, we access realms that can transform us at both singular and universal levels. We recognize the truth of who we are, and we can step into our birthrights as ambassadors for higher vibrational beings.

As you believe and trust, hope rises within your heart. To fully awaken to our spiritual selves, we need to tap into the wisdom that resides deep within. Embracing these waves of faith will empower us to seek sacred knowledge beyond material reality. Step into the higher frequencies of love as we prepare for this post-pandemic world.

The genesis of my connections to angels had begun with a medical miracle. A miracle sits on the edge between what we know and the unknowable. It's the incomprehensible, the mysterious that cannot be explained by physical laws. Yet miracles give us hope and drive us to create reality out of possibility.

With the onset of the spontaneous healing of my vocal cord, I had to accept there was more to life than meets the eye; I know it to be true. I now understand my miraculous healing had opened my communications with angels.

Now, I ask you to believe. Accept what you cannot see and have faith that you are part of an angelic blueprint into a new Earth. Don't search for miracles out there, but go within, for that's how it begins. Listen to the wisdom of your heart and accept there could be something that connects us with the cosmic memory that unites us all.

As your heart opens, you might start hearing the whispers of angels as they beckon you to come closer. Trust in them, and let them be your guiding light, showing the way. Allow the angels to lead this mystical dance into the ethers of the unknown. Let us cross the threshold of our new horizon with our angels, together, as one. Let love lead the way.

BONUS:
HEAVENLY HELP
FROM THE RELUCTANT MESSENGER

The raging storm had knocked out the electricity. "Maybe the darkness will help me hide," I thought as I cowered in the corner of my closet and tried to silence my rapid breathing. This vivid and terrifying nightmare continued as my thoughts begged over and over, "Please don't let him find me." I should have grabbed my cell phone from the bedside table when I heard him break in. I was terrified. How did he get in? The power outage must have deactivated the alarm. Nothing good could come from this, and I did not see any way to escape. I feared for my life. I felt desperate, powerless. There were evil forces set against me, and the only thing I could do was pray.

This hellish nightmare had its genesis three days earlier, on March 25, 2014, with the most innocent circumstance. I had attended a midnight meditation. The weather had turned cold, which was probably the reason why only four came to this outdoor ceremony. While meditating, I felt uncomfortable; something did not seem right. I opened my eyes and was surprised to see that the man next to me was staring in my direction and smiling. I closed my eyes and returned to the meditation. What did he want? Why the stare? Why the smile? It unnerved me.

The next day he called and emailed me several times, so any doubts I might have had about his intentions were gone. When I informed him that I had no interest in any further communications, it seemed to enrage him, and his attempts to contact me escalated. I blocked his phone calls and emails, but that didn't deter him.

When conventional methods failed to reach me, he used a different and even more terrifying tactic: he contacted me psychically. I sensed his presence when I was alone. I felt him near me when I was at work. I would turn around expecting to see him, but no one would be there. He invaded my dreams.

I did not record the details of the nightmare in my dream journal; I did not want to think about it, much less document it. I simply summarized it as "disturbing," and I ended the entry with this sentence: "I have to set up protections to keep him out of my dream space."

Set up protections? On one level I knew I needed to do that, but how? I felt overwhelmed, and I didn't know how to proceed. These feelings of helplessness brought me back to the nightmare, cowering in the corner of my closet, terrified as I hid from this predator, and prayed for help.

My journey to the unknown had changed me. With each message, I grew more sensitive as I learned to use my nonphysical senses to help expand my awareness. I had become more empathetic and understanding. My increased sensitivity to the surrounding subtle energies allowed me to experience the extraordinary while still living in an ordinary world, but this sensitivity had its downside. I had become vulnerable to negative energy.

I had learned from previous messengers about energy associated with emotions. Negative energy accompanied emotions such as jealousy, envy, or anger. When these emotions were directed at others, negative energy was sent in that direction, and this occurred whether it was intentional or not. Any negative or low energy directed at others could have debilitating results, and the more sensitive the recipient, the more profound the effects. These attacks have the potential to change a person on physical as well as emotional levels.

A number of websites[28] list common signs and symptoms of negative energy attacks, including feeling fatigued for no discernable reason, having weakness or stabbing pains in specific areas (such as the chest or upper back), and emotional reactions such as depression, sleep disturbances, irritability, anxiety, and, as I had learned through personal experience, nightmares.

I had heard of psychic attacks, but I never expected to experience them. In response to my plea, help arrived at the end of March. As I began to dictate the message, I realized my voice sounded different: it was soft and gentle. A change in voice quality was often an indicator that a new messenger had arrived.

March 29, 2014

We were watching in observance while this one participated in the meditation ceremony. It is always with protection and love that we surround her, as we did during this time.

Her thoughts are correct; the meditation was hijacked by the interfering energies of the one known as [name deleted]. [Name deleted] went beyond ethical considerations and attempted to interfere with this one's experience. We were there as a protective shield. During the meditation, this one perceived an energy field wrapped around her. This was a shield we put in place. We layered our protective energies around her.

---

28 thoughtco.com/what-is-a-psychic-attack-1730541

This was true; I had felt a force field that surrounded me during the meditation. In my mind's eye, I had seen a webbed matrix wrapped around my body that insulated me like a warm blanket.

From her left side, she saw negative energies approaching. This is the side where he was. Our protection prevented the negative energies from manifesting. Those negative energies were brought on by the malcontent of this man. Because of the energy field we had set forth, he did not cause harm to this, our beloved one. We continued to maintain a shield from him as he persisted in his attempts to gain this one's attention.

Another event of this sort, without his interfering energy, will result in very different outcomes, for this one will be able to soar and make further connections. This one is wise in continuing to protect her space during the dream state. We, too, will add protections for her.

I love outdoor midnight meditations, surrounded by the stillness of the evening, the sounds of nature, and only stars and the moon for lighting. I am disconnected from all electronics: no ringing phones, chiming texts, or televisions blaring. It is easy to forget about the day's worries and focus on connecting to nature and the universe.

This time, however, I did not experience any connections; I felt disappointed because nothing happened. With the exception of the mental image of the webbed matrix that covered me, nothing out of the ordinary occurred. There were no contemplative insights; in fact, the only thoughts I had were of the cold temperatures and my desire to go home.

Learning about the *"protective shield"* from the messenger changed my perspective. Although the matrix protected me from this man's negative energies, it also prevented me from experiencing any positive benefits. Suddenly, it all made sense. No wonder nothing happened.

I had pondered how to shield myself from this man during my dream state, and this message provided the answers. Just as the image of a cage of energy had protected me during the ceremony, I could do the same for myself during my dreams, but first I needed to review a couple of older messages.

Previous communications had disclosed that energy follows thought, and action follows energy. So, if I imagined a barrier around myself, I would be engaging the energy of protection. I could do this, but I felt comforted to know I would have assistance. The message continued:

> *There have been past lives with the one named* [name deleted]. *At one time, he had been a very powerful sorcerer. He used his powers for good as well as darkness. Deep within his heart, he continues his search for power which he is seeking from this one, our beloved. She now has the tools to return to earlier lifetimes with* [name deleted]. *As she does this, she can block the energies and alter the previous patterns established with* [name deleted] *in different lifetimes that are now affecting her.*

This communication required me to review another set of messages about Points of Existence and expanded consciousness. As a person's awareness increases, more waves of the timeline are incorporated within the stretched Point of Existence. There is direct correlation between the number of sine waves enclosed within the Point of Existence and the likelihood of the person experiencing distortions in normally experienced time. This is the point when both future and past lives can be accessed.

I had never given much thought to past lives, so these instructions to enter the space of expanded awareness to change events through past lives left me feeling confused. Could I do this? I didn't know if I could, but I wanted to stop these negative energy attacks.

I had collected various tools to help me on my journey to the unknown. I had learned several methods to stretch my Point of Existence in order to enter a state of expanded awareness. In addition to the more conventional methods such as meditation, prayer, and deep breathing, I had learned about using my Emotional Guidance System to increase the energy frequency surrounding my body. Having a "lighter" energy field made expanded awareness an easier state to achieve. I had also learned how to reduce brain chatter by visualization, using the formula that energy follows thought, and action follows energy.

Whether or not I endorsed the concept of past lives didn't matter. I would enter a state of expanded awareness. From there I would connect to this man's energy and set an intention to alter any previous vibrational patterns to make changes in this current time. Theoretically this sounded straightforward; I hoped I could do it.

Until then, I would ignore any skepticism I might have about past lives, and I would just proceed on my journey. No sense dwelling on ideology; I had to take care of this—the sooner, the better.

The lessons she learned during the meditation did not appear significant to her, but we gave her the tools she needed to deal with the situation with the one named [name deleted]. *We helped guide her to the tools she needed to thwart the energies of* [name deleted]. *This one's situation that needed healing involved current, past, and future protection from the one named* [name deleted]. *She now has the ability to protect herself.*

Lessons learned? This proved to be true. Initially I had

walked away from the meditation more than a little disappointed. Although I did not understand it at the time, the sage words of the messenger made me realize how valuable the meditative experience had actually been. Not only had I been protected during the ceremony, but also enlightened. The manner in which the messengers shielded me became another tool for future use. It also opened the door to connect with what I now believe are divine, heavenly energies.

As she continues her path, we will become more open to her. There will be a brief cessation of awareness of dreams and messages due to the continual vigilance from us as we shield her from the energies of [name deleted]. *When we recognize his energies are no longer a threat, there will be an allowance of further energies and information which she seeks.*

She is to rest and know she is loved beyond measure, and she is protected. This protection results in a blocking of messages at the current time. She is now aware of this, and she will welcome the time when she is totally protected, and then the messages will flow again.

I felt reassured to learn of the protections put in place during the initial psychic attack. Adding protections during meditations and dreams would temporarily halt the messages. Nevertheless, I would do anything to stop these attacks.

What had begun as a desperate plea for help resulted in contact with these divine beings from the angelic realm. Once opened, this door allowed for further communication.

I heard from them again four days later. It was on a Wednesday, the first week following spring break. Although I am usually awake and out of bed a few minutes before the alarm rings, I was still operating on "spring break time," and the alarm shattered my deep sleep. I jumped out of bed and immediately took a shower to help me stay awake. While in the shower, I began to receive a message. I toweled off and grabbed my phone to record the message.

As I began my dictation, I noticed a change in my voice, and I felt calm and at total peace—quite different than what I had felt just moments before. I now associate this sense of tranquility with messengers from the angelic realm.

April 2, 2014

There are protections in place for this one. She is aware of other energies with her during the meditation ceremony. These are the energies of protection and guidance that have been with her throughout her lifetime. With this comes love and deep appreciation for the learning that has taken place in this lifetime. We have been vigilant in our protections of this one, just waiting for her awareness of us.

This energy is one of gratitude and grace as well as love. Now that the door to this energy field has opened, this one will be able to tap into this field when it is needed. It is as if her heart has discovered an additional chamber, allowing more to flood into her awareness.

We have always been with her and will remain so. This one thinks the energy is one of angelic proportion. Those are concepts humans have used to describe our energies. It is a good analogy to describe our energy fields and vibratory signatures.

As I dictated the message, I had an overwhelming feeling of being surrounded by a host of holy beings, from whom emanated grace, serenity, and peace. I felt encompassed by pure love.

The key is to ask. We have always been here but have been awaiting your request for assistance.

216

It felt empowering to know this energy had always been available, awaiting my request. I could sense the connection, as if a stream of energy had begun to flow to me from the angelic realm. I first saw my body fill with beautiful, soft, pink energy. It felt like I had walked into a bank of pink fog, and a sense of euphoria washed over me.

I knew my request had started a chain of energy events to make the connection possible. Help is always there; all I need to do is ask. In a download of information, the angels told me I had become a beacon, and this new energy would attract a different set of people to me. This guiding light would draw in those who needed the energy of peace and calm into their lives. The angels instructed me to wait and observe responses from other people, and so I did.

I was vigilant for the next several days, and the results were remarkable. I am all business at work, and I rarely take time for idle chat, so it is unusual for people to come by to say hello. However, over the next few days, my office seemed like it had a revolving door. In three days, I had more social visits than I'd had the previous three months combined. Even more interesting, most of these people had never been to my office before.

For example, Juliet, a physical therapist who had begun working at this elementary school eight months before, stopped by my office. I was sitting at my computer, working on a psychological report, when I heard a light tapping at my open door. I looked up and welcomed Juliet in. As she greeted me with her lovely British accent, she walked to my chair and leaned down to give me a quick kiss on the top of my head. It was a kind gesture, but certainly unusual, especially for her first visit to my office.

The next day I drove to the school district's administrative center for a meeting. As I got out of my car, I saw the principal of a school where I had previously worked. During my tenure at that school, our exchanges had never been personal. Today, however, she walked across the parking lot and greeted me with a big hug and friendly conversation. I smiled, not only at her reaction, but also at the validation it brought from the angels. As instructed, I had waited and observed. The angels were right; a different set of people had been drawn to my energy. I was becoming a believer.

I received more messages from the angelic realm about six weeks later. The following message brought me back in time to 1966.

May 13, 2014

We are a set of energies here to guide and protect you. Our doors have been open to you for many years, such as the time you almost stepped on a snake and we pulled you away from danger. This happened over fifty Earth years ago, and we now remind you of this event. You have told many people of this story.

A vision transported me back in time to my adolescent years. I walked barefooted through a field of tall grass, searching the 400-acre farm for my horse. With my horse's bridle slung over my left shoulder, I felt the cool grass beneath my bare feet. The warm sun beat down on my back in contrast to a gentle breeze that cooled my head and neck. I felt my ponytail swinging as I walked the fields.

From the perspective of both observer and participant, the speed of this internal video changed to slow motion. I walked with my head held high, and as I peered into the distance to locate my horse, something made me look down. My bare foot was inches from a large, multicolored, coiled snake.

Then it happened. It felt as if an invisible set of hands grabbed my shoulders, lifted me into the air, and pulled me away from the danger. Even now, my heart races as I think about the coiled snake within inches of my bare foot.

I remembered telling family and friends about this event. As I was stepping down, something had made me look at the ground. What had it been? When I flew up in the air, away from the snake, I had theorized it was my guardian angel who had protected me. Now, more than fifty years later, the messenger confirmed my theory.

> *We represent a series of protective energies that have come into your consciousness, just as other energy systems have. This is due to your continued state of expanded awareness.*
>
> *Although some humans perceive us as hovering above, most humans are unaware of us. Mother Earth is transitioning, and over the past twenty or more years, the awareness of our existence has increased. The popularity of angels is because many from our realm are now being perceived by humans. We have not reached into their conscious awareness; it is just the opposite. The awareness of many humans, partially due to Mother Earth's transition, has expanded and has broached into our dimension.*
>
> *Much like the attraction of a bright, sparkling light, our energies are beacons for some humans. Some can perceive the subtle energy frequencies of our realm and are thus attracted to us.*
>
> *We are happy this one is aware of her ability to call upon various energy sources such as ours. We will demonstrate to her our existence today. We know that she does not need this proof, but we do this from the energy of love. Today we shall be with her in an obvious, apparent manner. Her day will be filled with small examples that are influenced by our energies.*

This message seemed similar to the previous month's demonstration of how others would be drawn to me as a beacon of light, and I felt eager to see what would happen this time. As soon as I dictated the last paragraph into my voice recorder, I found myself taking a deep, cleansing breath that seemed to settle throughout my entire body, filling me with a sense of peace and happiness. I realized this intake of breath allowed the energies from the angels' realm to enter. I began to smile as I beamed with this new energy.

Throughout the day I experienced more acts of kindness and compassion from others than I had for months. Although there were no events of monumental importance, the day filled with multiple examples of the angels' presence. Strangers met me with smiles and some with conversations. Drivers were thoughtful and considerate. The cashier at the grocery store started talking with me about the importance of gratitude. If only every day could be like this!

Later that evening as I was putting on my pajamas and getting my work clothes out for the next day, I felt a mental nudge. I stopped and took a deep breath. From seemingly out of nowhere, I realized it was only two days until my late husband's birthday. A memory from September 2, 1987, the day Daryl died, came flooding into my awareness:

While in the hospital's ICU waiting room, I had overheard a man telling his friend he had seen an angel several years before. An angel had appeared next to him on a busy street corner in Cincinnati, Ohio. It then flew in front of him and into the sky. He chuckled as he told his friend that the angel had wings on his feet.

I left the waiting room a few minutes later to return to Daryl's bedside. When the hospital's chaplain entered the room, I asked for prayers to help release my husband from his pain. Daryl was in a coma, and I knew he was ready to leave.

I took the chaplain's proffered hand, and we each placed a hand on Daryl. As I closed my eyes, I felt a deep sense of peace as I listened to the chaplain's heartfelt prayer. Then I heard him call for the "angels with winged feet" to carry Daryl home. I had never heard of angels with winged feet, but twice within the same hour made me a believer, and I knew the angels with winged feet would carry Daryl to his heavenly home. A short time later, Daryl took his last breath.

When I shared this story with my sister Eleanore, she told me the men in the waiting room were the angels in human form. She reminded me of the Bible verse in Hebrews 13:2: "Be not forgetful to entertain strangers: for thereby, some have entertained angels unaware."

The following message came as I reminisced:

Yes, we were there, and we were able to manifest in full physical form as humans, a form you could not only see but hear, for you needed to hear the words that were shared. Our full manifestations were needed, an ever-present reminder that life continues when the Earth form drops away. We manifested in physical forms in order to escort your beloved to our realm. Your ability to see us, hear us, and remember us was partially due to the close connection you had and continue to have with your husband, even when the physical body is gone. Nothing changes. The true essence continues to live on.

The angels were there in human form, waiting to escort Daryl to his heavenly home. Even more important, they verified the truth that love transcends the physical: true essence continues and does not die. The angels had fulfilled their promise of making their earlier presence known to me today, by sharing both a fifty-year-old incident, when I had been a teenager, and their presence with me, when Daryl had died twenty-seven years ago.

I had a vivid dream of angels about a year later, in May 2015. The setting in the dream was a Victorian-style house. I was in a bedroom, dressed in a long, white, flowing cotton nightgown, and I was floating about two or three feet off the ground.

Several angels floated in slow circles around me while I was suspended in midair; they blew their breath on me like whispers in the wind. I looked down and saw a tube of medicine on a bedside table. I recognized it as medicinal salve by its metallic silver cover, black screw cap, and label. One word was printed on the label: *Seraphim*. This was a healing balm created by seraphim angels.

When I woke the next morning, I found myself singing the chorus of an old spiritual song: "All night, all day, angels watching over me, my Lord. All night, all day, angels watching over me." Messages began pouring in; I retrieved my phone and recorded the following:

May 12, 2015

This one attuned to the energy of angels which allowed for contact during the dream state. This one felt angels gently blowing on her body. It is similar to a tender breeze that blows across a field of flowers. That breeze is the breath from Mother Earth herself. It comes from within her heart.

The breath this one experienced during her dream state came from angels. Just as with Mother Earth, the breath of angels also comes from the heart. It can be perceived through the body's senses, but the true perception, the perception of truth, comes when it is perceived by the heart. It is the heart that is the most sensitive organ in the human body. Perceiving through the heart is what allowed this one to recognize and acknowledge the presence of the angels.

Communication with angels occurs on a higher vibratory level, and thus it is more difficult to perceive. When humans enter a state of silence and stillness, their antennae become alerted to the more sensitive vibrations from angels. This is why our presence is often felt or acknowledged during prayer, meditation, or the dream state, for these are times when humans have entered into a higher vibratory level and are able to attune to our frequencies.

Although this one referred to seraphim, we say the name of the angel or type of angel is not as important to us as it is to humans. The name is the vibratory signature of the specific angel. Everything is energy. When the name is spoken, there is an energy vibration from the vocal cords. Those energy vibrations leave the human's body and are received by another human's ears. The energy waves vibrate in the human's ears. The human's brain translates those energies to sound. Thus, when an angel's name is spoken aloud, the name is the specific vibratory frequency connected with that angel.

The name of the angel is not as important as the energy frequency itself. Of course, there are other ways in which the signature energy frequencies can be registered. Not only can it be registered as sound as just described, but also through other human senses such as sight, touch, or smell. For those humans who are more sensitive, the signature may be recognized by a knowing or by using the "non-senses."

As soon as I recorded the message, I looked at the time. I could briefly search online about seraphim angels and about the spiritual meanings of *breath* before I got ready for work.

According to the Jewish Encyclopedia website, the seraphim are mentioned in the Christian Bible, the Book of Enoch, and the Torah.[29] Although I should have been accustomed to these uncanny synchronistic findings, what I read surprised me: The

29 jewishencyclopedia.com/articles/13437-seraphim

seraphim have wings on their feet! They have six wings: two to cover their faces, two for flying, and two that cover their feet. Years later, I learned they were the angels with winged feet at the hospital when my husband had died so many years before.

In Revelation 4:8, the six-winged seraphim angels are described as unceasingly singing the praises of the Lord God, the Almighty, day and night. The phrase "day and night" caught my attention, and its similarity to the "All night, all day" lyrics I had sung when I had awakened from the dream with the seraphim.

I continued my search and learned that the breath is mentioned in many religious and philosophical doctrines. The Christian New Testament and the Hebrew Bible, or Old Testament, have several references to breath, indicating this is how the Almighty gives life (Job 33: 4). Hindu philosophy refers to receiving "prana," or life-force energy, from the breath.[30] What mystical and sacred qualities were in the breath of angels in my dream?

I received a follow-up message to the dream about the seraphim angels a couple weeks later. Summer break was a few days away, and I could hardly wait. As I daydreamed one morning about how to spend my summer vacation, a message demanded to be heard. I picked up my phone and captured this message:

May 28, 2015

We came to this one in a dream about the breath of angels, for the energy we put forth is very subtle. It is a lighter, finer energy than a gentle breath, just as a gentle breath is lighter and finer than a whisper, and a whisper is lighter than speaking, and speaking is lighter than shouting. As this one continues to fine-tune her senses and tap into the realm of non-senses, she will be able to discern the differences among us.

There are many types of beings within our realm—the realm

---

30 hinduwebsite.com/hinduism/concepts/prana.asp

humans refer to as the angelic realm. There is the energy of the Protector. Humans associate this subset of the angelic realm with the archangel called Michael. He is considered the leader or head of this realm.

There is also a subset for healing which humans associate with the archangel named Raphael. The energy of the Healers is different from the Protectors. There are multiple subsets within the angelic realm such as the Guardian subset. We also have a section for Awareness. It has a similar energy to the Protectors, but it is gentler.

Let us now speak of common features among the angelic realm. We are beings of higher vibrations than are found on the Earth plane. Our vibrational frequencies are subtler and finer. We respond to like energy such as when humans tap into our energy field. Many humans know in order to gain assistance from us, they need to ask for help.

We are always around, but we rarely interfere with the day to day "busyness" of life on the Earth plane unless we are asked to do so. It is the asking or the intent that sends forth an energy beacon from the human to our realm. The asking, in the form of intentions and prayers, is energy. These are of a higher vibrational frequency which more closely matches our vibrations. The energy vibrations reach the interface, the area that buffers our realm of existence from that of the humans. If the request is from the heart, the energy reaches us like a knock upon our door. We respond to like energy; when the request is from the heart, this energy reaches us like a small, brilliant spark of light that flashes.

When a prayer or intention is genuine, that energy stems from the heart. It is the heart energy of humans that represents the higher vibrational status needed in order for connections to be made into our dimension.

I saw myself in a large, cool, damp, cave in my mind's eye. Total blackness surrounded me; natural light could not enter this underground cavern. I saw a single match spark to life, and its light permeated the cave. My view changed, zooming backward, and the cave increased in size tenfold. I watched another match ignite, and as before, light filled the cave.

When there is darkness, the light of a single match is bright enough to be seen for miles; it is a call for attention. Our prayers or requests for help are our angelic beacons. Though small, our lights have enough luminous intensity to reach the angels' realm. The message continued:

The angel realm is a subset of one of the new sets of rays from your sun. Review that information. Similar to a rainbow or the chakra system, the seven rays range in color, and each color has its own vibrational frequency. The angel realm vibrates at a very high frequency level.

As requested, I reviewed the previous messages about the seven rays in the sun as outlined in Chapter 5: Cosmic Contacts. According to this new correspondence, the angel realm resides within one of those new columns of light.

Within each ray of energy, there are subsets, a microcosm of the macrocosm. Each of those rays is further divided into seven realms which correspond to different angels with specific frequency patterns that are associated with what humans refer to as skill sets or jobs. Humans frequently associate various archangels with specific colors due to the color pattern or vibration from their Source of existence.

When I searched "colors associated with archangels" online, many sites reported that not only were specific colors associated

226

with different respective archangels, but so were gemstones. I also learned about a metaphysical system of angel colors based on seven different rays of light. (There's that number seven again!) The website reported that each color vibrates at a different electromagnetic energy frequency, and specific angels are associated with each specific frequency[31] —the same information I had learned from the angels. By this time I expected to be accustomed to these eerie findings, but I wasn't. Even now, each time I validate information that had come to me from "nowhere," I am filled with a sense of wonder and excitement.

The energy from the angels felt unlike anything I had ever known. I experienced a sense of comfort knowing they were always with me, and I felt empowered when I learned to call on them. I no longer waited for extreme conditions; I had learned to ask them for assistance during many day-to-day activities: protection while driving, compassion while working with upset parents, strength and energy to complete a long week's work.

More than three years later, as I checked various upcoming spiritual classes in my area, one called "Angel Channeling" piqued my interest. I decided to attend. In June 2015, I drove to East Naples to Unity of Naples Church. I was glad that I had GPS, because the church is tucked back from the road in a beautifully wooded lot that surrounds a lake. As I parked my car and headed toward the building, I felt a sense of peace and serenity. It was as if this church rested on hallowed grounds.

I entered Fellowship Hall at Unity Church of Naples and took a seat, waiting for the class to begin. Information flooded into my awareness from the angel realm. I pulled out my notebook and started writing as fast as I could.

31 thoughtco.com/angel-colors-light-rays-of-angels-123826

June 18, 2015

The energy of angels is subtle, much like the soft, gentle mist emanating from the water of a babbling brook or the mist surrounding raindrops falling from the sky. It is not the energy of the water, but instead that almost imperceptible energy of the mist that surrounds the water or rain. The energy from our realm, the angel realm, is subtle, and therefore requires recognition in order for a connection to be made. This recognition can be found within a prayer, an intention, meditation, or just a simple wish. We are always present, awaiting your recognition of us.

As loved ones enter this most sacred and beloved space, we begin to gather together, and we surround each beloved one with the golden light from our Maker. There is a hush, a sense of reverence that falls upon this sacred circle as we soften the edges of concerns and worries some of these loved ones have. We enter their energy fields, and we fill those gaps with loving, divine light.

A vision accompanied the words, and I saw myself at the church while also standing in a densely wooded forest. I looked up and saw thousands of miniature stars. The sky began to fall, and these golden sparkles descended on me like a gentle mist. As pastel pink and green bands of energy gently wove back and forth in this haze of golden glitter, the tiny flecks of light began to twinkle as if awakening from a deep slumber. The energy blanketed the room where the twenty-seven participants were seated in a semicircle.

Our energy helps our loved ones breathe a little easier and deeper. As our loved ones breathe in, they take in this beautiful energy we share with this beloved group.

We see the energy of the group begin to ascend toward our realm, thus beginning to raise the veil separating our dimensions. As this sacred group's energy is lifted, even more angels from our realm descend into this room. It is with total love that we welcome this energy. It is with respect and gratitude that we acknowledge each and every precious soul in attendance. Welcome, beloved ones.

The words of the message and the images of the pastel ribbons of energy floating among blinking sparkles of light brought me to tears. This powerful yet serene energy helps *"soften the edges of concerns and worries"* by entering our energy fields and filling our *"gaps with loving, divine light."* This accurately described my own feeling; it was as if the angels reached deep inside me to touch my soul.

The group's intention sent forth an energy invitation for angels to connect. As they answered our calls, vibrational entrainment occurred, and the frequency signature of the prayer, meditation, or intention became synchronized with angelic vibratory patterns. This opened the door for future contact because it raised the veil separating our dimensions. The results strengthen when the prayer or meditation occurs in a group.

The collective power of group energy magnifying prayers is not a new concept. Matthew 18:20 states, "For where two or three are gathered together in my name, there am I in the midst of them." The collective energy of the meditation group combined with the sacred grounds of Unity Church set the stage for powerful and profound spiritual experiences. We were primed and ready to receive the healing energies from the angels and the loving messages shared by Gigi Petersen, a gifted psychic who channeled the sacred words from the angels. Although I did not know any of the participants beforehand, I had become part of their family before the meditation had ended. I felt a sense of harmony and unity not only with my brothers and sisters in the group but also with others throughout the world. The presence and messages from the angels confirmed we were not separate; we were part of the sacred connection to all that is.

An angelic presence fills the heart with love and joy. Angels surround us and guard us, but they often work behind the scenes. They have been with me throughout my life, protecting me as a teen by pulling me away from a coiled snake. Wrapping their wings around me, they shielded me from people who wished to harm me. Angels have visited in dreams, spoken through messages, and manifested in full physical form as humans in a time of great need in my life.

My life has been blessed and enriched by angels. Their presence is pervasive; they are always watching and ready to heed our cries for help. Angels were here when we entered the world, and they will accompany us when it is our time to exit. Their willingness to come to our aid brings us solace even in our darkest hours, offering peace, protection, and serenity. It is a comfort to know we are never alone.

ACKNOWLEDGMENTS

I have to start by thanking my family. I could not have written this book without your support. To my son, Phillip, you encouraged me to write from my heart. You kept me on my toes with your latest theories about the mysteries of the universe. My daughter, Cassie, you inspire me with your endless energy as you balance all aspects of life with grace. You lead by example, showing your girls the importance of family.

I want to thank my son-in-law, Dan, and my daughter-in-law, Kelly. You two are the perfect companions for Cassie and Phillip, and I could not love you more than if you had been my own. Dan, I watch as you work so hard, day in and day out, yet you always have time for Cassie and the girls. Your devotion as a husband and father inspires me. Kelly, you are one of the most creative, talented women I know. You amaze me. With the singing voice of an angel, you spread joy to all who hear you. I wholeheartedly thank both of you for making my children happy and complete.

To my granddaughters, Lorelai and Shalane, you have no idea of the impact you have had on my life. Where has the time gone? With your eighth and fourth birthdays just around the corner, I marvel how you've both grown. You give me a reason to laugh, to celebrate, to play. Most importantly, you give me hope for the future. You have added such richness to my already full life; I don't know where I'd be without you.

Eleanore, not only are you an awesome sister, but you helped me more than you can imagine. After reading my early drafts, you saved me from several grammatical errors that would have made my college English professors cringe. Thank you so much for your watchful eye.

I wish to thank Monroe Institute in Virginia for providing me with training wheels to explore the universe. You taught me I am more than my physical body, and your programs opened doors to nonphysical realms, allowing me to communicate with angelic beings. Thank you for being there for me.

Reverend Renee Bledsoe, you supported me, guided me on my spiritual path, offering a safe haven when I needed it. Church of Spiritual Light has become my home away from home. Thank you for sharing your wisdom, my sister in spirit.

Beth Brown-Rinella, from our first meeting, I knew we were connected. Thank you for providing meditations that magically speak to my soul. I am so happy I found Goddess I Am. I never thought I'd find a mecca for spiritual seekers in the heart of Naples. I'm proud to call you my friend.

Sandra McGill and Lee Shook, I'll never forget my adventures during the angel washes. Thank you for your insight in developing such a fantastic tool for all to use. Sandra, I'll always be grateful for your wisdom that helped guide angels into my life.

I offer special thanks to Maryna Zhukova at www.marydes. eu. You worked your wonder, once again, to provide the perfect book cover and interior design. I'm deeply indebted to you and the magic you bring into your work.

I am grateful for those who contacted me after reading my first book, *The Reluctant Messenger*. The personal stories you've shared have touched my heart, and it makes my author journey worthwhile. I especially want to thank Keith, Jenn, Mark, Linda, Cari, Joe, Steve, Kelly, Christine, Ken, Donna, Brie, Debbie, Lizbeth,

Byron, and Dan. Thank you for the support you've shown me. Know I hold a special place in my heart for each of you.

Last but not least, I thank Clark Press and The Muses Within for making sense of my mystical musings as I traveled this mysterious cosmos of the unseen. Thank you for your guidance in the world of social platforms. I've tweeted, posted, and uploaded more than I thought was possible. Although I kicked and screamed at having a YouTube channel, I now understand your sage advice. I appreciate your patience and understanding. Thank you for believing in me.

Made in United States
Orlando, FL
12 September 2022

22323562R00146